Do Parents Know They Matter?

WITHDRAWN

2 0 JUN 2023

D0277399

Also available from Continuum

Pocket PAL: Involving Parents in Schools, B. Lucas

Learn to Transform, D. Crossley and G. Corbyn

Improving Schools in Exceptionally Challenging Circumstances, A. Harris, P. Clarke, S. James, J. Gunraj and B. James

School Effectiveness and School Improvement, A. Harris and N. Bennett

Do Parents Know They Matter?

Raising Achievement through Parental Engagement

Alma Harris,
Kirstie Andrew-Power
and Janet Goodall

YORK ST. JOHN
LIBRARY & INFORMATION
SERVICES

continuum

Continuum International Publishing Group

The Tower Building	80 Maiden Lane, Suite 704
11 York Road	New York,
London SE1 7NX	NY 10038

www.continuumbooks.com

© Alma Harris, Kirstie Andrew-Power and Janet Goodall 2009

First published 2009
Reprinted 2010

All rights reserved. No part of this publication may be reproduced or transmitted in any form or by any means, electronic or mechanical, including photocopying, recording, or any information storage or retrieval system, without prior permission in writing from the publishers.

Alma Harris, Kirstie Andrew-Power and Janet Goodall have asserted their right under the Copyright, Designs and Patents Act, 1988, to be identified as Authors of this work.

British Library Cataloguing-in-Publication Data
A catalogue record for this book is available from the British Library.

ISBN: 9781855394797 (paperback)

Library of Congress Cataloging-in-Publication Data

Do parents know they matter? : raising achievement through parental engagement/ Alma Harris, Kirstie Andrew-Power, and Janet Goodall.
    p. cm.
  Includes bibliographical references.
  ISBN 978-1-85539-479-7
1. Education–Parent participation. I. Andrew-Power, Kirstie. II. Goodall, Janet, 1957– III. Title.

  LB1048.5.H375 2008
  371.19′2–dc22

                                2008047251

Typeset by BookEns Ltd, Royston, Hertfordshire
Printed and bound in Great Britain by
CPI Antony Rowe, Chippenham, Wiltshire

Contents

Acknowledgements

The authors would like to thank and acknowledge the following individuals for their contribution to this book and their wider work on parental engagement:

David Crossley, Peter Wanless, John Dunford, Teresa Tunnadine, Tom Andrew-Power, Clare Foster, Louise Taylor, Jennifer Coupland, Daniel Evans, Rosanna Raimato, Rob Carter, Ani Magill, Charlotte Gormley, Mick O'Leary, Val Foster, Debbie Sheperd, Kelly Allen, Sarah Beanland, Carolyn Terry, Bridget Gibbs, Kate Emerson, Jane Ayshford and Alan Cowley.

Also the authors wish to acknowledge and thank the staff, students and parents from the following schools:

The Compton School, Alder Grange School, Hamstead Hall School, Greenford High School, The Kennet School, Longcroft School, St John the Baptist School, Sharnbrook Upper School, Cardinal Wiseman School, Carmel RC College, Shirelands Community College, Astley Community High School, Great Sankey School, Taverham High School, Cramlington High School, Bury Church of England High School, Chichester Boys School, The Warden Park School, Lytham St Annes Technology College, The Westwood School, Oakmeeds Community School, Chelmer Valley High School, Axton Chase School, The Headlands School, The Rising Brook College, Deptford Green School, Central Foundation Girls School, Bowring Community Sports College, Mount Carmel School, Kelvin Hall School, The Morton School, Feltham Community College, Westfield Community School, Sale Grammar School, Bushey Hall School, The Mirfield Free Grammar and Sixth Form College, Meole Brace School, Castle View School, Haling Manor High School, Pershore High School, Ramsay College, Bradley Stoke Community College, The

Cooper School, Cheadle Hume School, Romsey School, Etone Community School, Glenthorne High School, Oriel High School, Sion Manning RC Girls School, St John Bosco Arts College, Ashton Community Science College, John of Gaunt School, Fakenham High School, Weaverham School, St Anne's Catholic High School, Corpus Christi Catholic Sports College, The John Kyrle High School, The Gleed Girls' Technology College, The Belle Vue School, Stretford Grammar School, Campsmount Technology College, The City Academy Bristol, Hornsea School & Language College, Islington Arts & Media College, The Joseph Rowntree School, Salford City Academy, The Berry Hill High School, Millthorpe School, Wildern School, Chalfonts Community School, Hope Valley College, Warblington School, Slough Grammar School, Aston School, Riverside Business and Enterprise College, Sponne School, Willenhall School.

About the authors

Professor Alma Harris

Alma Harris is Pro-Director (Leadership) at the Institute of Education, London, and Chair in Educational Leadership at the London Centre for Leadership in Learning. She has previously held academic posts at the University of Warwick, University of Nottingham and University of Bath. She is also an Associate Director of the Specialist Schools and Academies Trust and editor of 'School Leadership and Management' (http://www.informaworld.com/SLandM).

Her research work has focused upon organizational change and development. She is internationally known for her work on school improvement, focusing particularly on ways in which leadership can contribute to school development and change. She is currently co-directing a large scale DCSF project on 'Leadership and Learning Outcomes' and an ESRC study on 'Multi-agency Leadership'.

Her writing has explored middle-level leadership, teacher leadership and leadership in challenging circumstances. Her most recent work has focused on parental engagement (Harris and Goodall 2007; 2008) and leadership in multi-agency contexts.

Kirstie Andrew-Power

Kirstie Andrew-Power is Head of Achievement at the Specialist Schools and Academies Trust and leads the 'Every Child Achieves' network of over 700 schools. The network focuses on maximizing outcomes for *every* learner and provides support and opportunities with literacy, behaviour, diversity and parental engagement. Kirstie led the 18-month national EPRA campaign (Engaging Parents in Raising Achievement).

In her first senior leadership post at The Compton School in Barnet, Kirstie held responsibility for student and professional learning and was a Lead Practitioner for Equality and Inclusion. She was responsible for teaching and learning and new technologies after promotion to Wildern School in Hampshire.

She has authored and contributed to wide-ranging publications on professional learning, equality and inclusion, engaging parents in raising achievement, behaviour, environments for learning and achievement of boys.

Dr Janet Goodall

Janet Goodall is a research fellow at the Institute of Education, University of Warwick. She was previously a research assistant in the School of Education at the University of Nottingham.

Her research work has focused on school improvement. She has worked with the Specialist Schools and Academies Trust in the EPRA project, and in relation to Workforce Reform. She has also been involved in NCSL research on networks of schools, as well as research for the (then) DfES pilot project on federations. While at Nottingham, her work focused on the Continuing Professional Development of Teachers.

Introduction

> ... if you've not had any engagement with your child's school then it can be daunting. You don't realise that you can have such a valuable input, even in just a small way.
>
> (Parent)

Across the world there is a growing recognition of the importance of engaging parents, families and communities in raising the educational aspirations and attainment of young people (DEECD 2008). There is increasing evidence that highlights how parental engagement in schooling positively influences student achievement and attainment (Desforges and Abouchaar 2003). Engaging parents in learning can significantly affect and alter the life chances of young people, particularly those located in the most deprived localities. Engaging parents in learning can positively affect educational achievement and ensure that the powerful connection between parental background and subsequent educational attainment is broken, so that more young people can succeed irrespective of their context.

Studies of sustained school improvement have highlighted that parent and school partnerships are a critical component of successful improvement. This is particularly true of schools in challenging circumstances where the social and economic odds are often stacked against young people. Schools that secure academic success with students from low socio-economic backgrounds tend to succeed chiefly through the support, engagement and partnerships between *schools, families and communities* (Chadwick 2004). The evidence is clear; engaging parents in supporting their children's learning can have a substantial and positive impact upon achievement. In summary, schools that engage parents in learning are also most likely to secure high levels of student performance.

Although engaging parents in learning is undoubtedly a commonly shared aspiration across all schools, it also brings many challenges. Developing and sustaining effective partnerships between the home, the community and the school is far from straightforward or easy. Our hectic 24/7 society means that many parents find balancing work and home difficult. The nature of work has shifted and the composition of families has changed.

There are more young people in society who are not living in the parental home. There are also many looked-after children who do not have the benefit of parental support. Such factors can create a great deal of stress and many young people face major difficulties even before they arrive at the school gate. For them, getting to school and remaining in school throughout the day is a significant achievement.

Economic hardship and complex living arrangements can place a huge degree of stress on family life. Many parents have multiple demands on their time and their resources. Juggling the demands of childcare and work can be a real challenge. The range and composition of parents in a single school varies considerably and it is clear that many parents are simply not able to support their children's learning as much as they would like. While this could be perceived as disinterest by the school, it is simply the case that for many parents the pressures of modern living are proving to be too great.

Clearly, not all parents are the same. However, they are often seen as one large homogeneous group and therefore parental engagement strategies tend not to be finely differentiated. Generic and overarching approaches to engaging parents are worthy, but they often discount the variability and diversity of the parental group. As a consequence, many well intentioned approaches aimed at involving parents in the school and engaging them in students' learning tend not to succeed because the range and variation of need within the parental group has not been adequately assessed or accommodated.

It is inevitable that some parents and parental groups tend to be more involved with schools than others. More socially and economically advantaged parents tend to be more comfortable in communicating with teachers and schools. They are often an articulate group who feel confident enough to talk with teachers and other professionals. They are also the parents most likely to be in full-time, professional employment and will therefore have less time to engage with the school, even though they can see the clear benefits of doing so. They may be 'time poor', which means that they can be absent from school events aimed at parents and have relatively little time at home to support their children's learning.

Those parents who are less socially and economically advantaged, particularly new immigrants, minorities and non-English language speakers also face difficulties in engaging with the school. Differences in language and culture operate as barriers to certain groups of parents who might want to help their child learn but find the English education system quite bewildering. Many schools understand this and are focusing their considerable energies on helping parents from other cultures and communities to decode the education system. They are actively seeking ways of engaging parents so that they feel secure and confident in the school environment. To be most effective, schools have to be a safe, supportive place for parents as well as students.

As the case studies in this book show, there are a variety of ways in which parents from a variety of backgrounds can engage with schools and many ways in which parents can be encouraged to feel comfortable within the school environment. Schools that successfully engage parents in learning tend to communicate with them openly, clearly and frequently. They also tend to offer a wide range of opportunities for parents to learn more about the school and for staff to learn more about parents. This *two way* communication is of central importance if trust and mutual respect between parents, teachers and students is to be achieved.

Parents from all backgrounds can succumb to a wide variety of pressures. Schools and teachers are also not immune to the stresses of everyday life. The pressures of inspection, testing and performance targets mean that many schools are chasing multiple priorities that compete for valuable time, energy and resources. This can cause staff to feel that with so many other demands on their time, engaging parents is not a top priority.

With everything else they need to do, many schools find that they simply cannot devote sufficient time and energy to engaging parents and keeping them engaged. Many schools make valiant efforts to get parents into school, to keep them informed and updated and to interest them in learning, but engaging them in student *learning*, in the long term, often proves to be more difficult. So on both sides there may be the desire to work more closely in partnership, but the day-to-day reality often means that achieving this can be challenging for both schools and parents.

The book

This book is about the relationship between parental engagement and student achievement. It has been written for school staff and parents as a guide to what we know about the impact of parental engagement on learning and what type of engagement works best. The book does not claim to be the definitive guide on parental engagement, as there is a wide literature on this subject and numerous authoritative texts that offer much deeper insights into this particular topic (see references).

Also, the book does not claim to offer 'silver bullet' advice about the optimum ways of engaging parents in student learning. If it did, you would be wise to stop reading this immediately. There is no 'quick fix' or easy solution to securing parents' engagement in student learning. It takes effort and time.

The main purpose of this book is to synthesize contemporary research evidence about parental engagement and learning (particularly that located in the 'Engaging Parents: Raising Achievement' project) and to highlight examples of effective contemporary practice in schools. The intention is to provide a guide to effective practice rather than a blueprint for action.

As the case studies in this book illuminate and illustrate, engaging parents in learning can be hard fought and hard won. There are no fail-safe tactics or strategies. Much depends on finding the right approach for the particular school context and the community it serves. Parental engagement in student learning is primarily secured through building positive, trusting and respectful relationships with parents and the wider community. Engaging parents requires long-term effort and considerable energy, on both sides. But the rewards are many and the resulting gains in student learning are significant.

The book is about the 'why, how and what' of parental engagement in student learning. It looks at why engaging parents in learning is so important. It draws upon recent research evidence to demonstrate the significant benefits that engaging parents in learning can bring. It also focuses on how schools are currently engaging parents and the effectiveness of various approaches through case studies of contemporary practice. In addition, the book focuses on the 'what' of parental engagement by highlighting those strategies that seem to make a positive difference to student learning and those approaches that are less likely to bring about any gains in achievement.

It is the case that many schools are involved in a wide range of activities with parents that have little impact on learning. The fundamental argument throughout this book is that parents have to engage with student learning *in the home* for any significant and sustained learning gains to occur. Hence, schools should be looking to maximize support for learning in the home as a top priority in any developmental activity aimed at engaging parents.

Other types of activities that bring parents into connection with the school may certainly be useful for relationship building and can reinforce trust, but such activities are unlikely to make any real difference to student learning outcomes. While social events, parents evening, visits and PTA activities can be a good way of cementing positive relationships with parents, it is doubtful they can do little more that underline and reinforce the importance of parental support for learning. To impact positively upon learning outcomes, parents have to engage with learning in a consistent way, *within the home environment*.

This is the harsh reality and will no doubt be unpalatable news for those schools who are working relentlessly to create opportunities to get parents into school. Clearly, involving parents in school-based events and activities, in this way, are both necessary and worthwhile. We are certainly not suggesting that these activities do not add value in a whole range of ways. However, it is clear that such activities will not impact on student learning outcomes unless there is some *direct* connection between those activities and learning in the home context. When partnerships between parents and schools are developed and sustained on the basis of supporting student learning in the home, improvement in learning outcomes is much more likely to occur.

The book is divided into six chapters. Each author leads on a different dimension of the book. Alma Harris leads on the research findings and evidence contained in Chapters 1, 2 and 6. Kirstie Andrew Power leads on the case studies and illustrations from the EPRA project in Chapters 3 and 4. Janet Goodall leads on the findings from the EPRA evaluation in Chapter 5.

The book is organized as follows:

- Chapter 1 sets the context and explores why parental engagement in learning is so important.
- Chapter 2 explores and synthesizes the available evidence, highlighting what we know about successful approaches to engaging parents in learning.

- Chapters 3 and 4 focus on the practical reality of engaging parents in learning by drawing on a wide range of examples from the EPRA project.
- Chapter 5 outlines the main findings from the EPRA research project. This research evidence offers contemporary insights into the relationship between parental engagement and achievement, and the chapter highlights 'what we know' about maximizing this relationship.
- Chapter 6 presents the future challenges that some schools face in forging closer links with an increasingly diverse population of parents. It argues that in a rapidly changing world, links between school, parent and community engagement will be needed more than ever, not only to secure the improved learning of young people, but to also secure their well-being and safety.

Scene-setting

Current context

The simplest and most profound way to understand the values of any society is through its education system. Is every child given an equal chance to learn, to develop their skills and knowledge? Are all children helped to succeed, irrespective of their starting point and background? In England, the gap between the academic performance of children of lower socio-economic status families and young people from the most affluent backgrounds is widening (Lipsett 2008). Although the academic performance of poor children has generally increased, over the past few years the achievement gap persists throughout schooling.

This pattern of underperformance among certain groups is pervasive and seems resilient to change. Socio-economic differences remain a powerful predictor of subsequent educational achievement. Certain groups of students consistently fail to reach their potential while other groups consistently succeed. Children from low income families do not on average overcome the hurdle of lower initial attainment associated with socio-economic hardship. Differences in ethnicity, gender, class and economic well-being affect children long before they start school and have a powerful continuing influence as they get older.

Socio-economic status explains more than *half* the variation in student achievement, and low family income in childhood years makes a significant difference to subsequent educational outcomes. Part of the reason for the decline in social mobility in many countries is the strong bond between low levels of family income and subsequent educational attainment. The bond between social background and educational achievement is a powerful and persistent one.

Study after study highlights how students who live in extreme poverty fall well below international averages across a wide range of measures (Berliner 2006). Children with low or average socio-economic status (SES) tend to have better educational outcomes if they attend a school with high average SES. If they attend a school where the mix is predominantly low SES they are unlikely to make as much progress. In short, the social composition and the context of the school matters significantly in terms of subsequent student attainment and achievement. So, effective schools can and do make a difference.

The nature, extent and degree of parental support for education can offset many of the negative influences of growing up in a poor community. It is possible to 'buck the trend' of performance associated with SES, but this cannot be achieved by the school alone. Parents are a crucial and vital component in reversing the pervasive influence of SES on achievement. Schools that succeed in engaging families from very diverse backgrounds share three key practices. They:

- focus on building trusting collaborative relationships among teachers, families, and community members
- recognize, respect, and address families' needs, as well as class and cultural difference
- embrace a philosophy of partnership where power and responsibility are shared.

In short, the support of parents for learning and achievement is the single most important contributory factor to increased student achievement. In terms of raising school performance, parents matter significantly.

Parents matter

The extent to which 'parents matter' means that parental engagement is once again at the epicenter of policy-making in a range of countries. In England, government guidelines for improving the provision for children and young people have been introduced in the form of the 'Children's Plan'. This Plan outlines a strategy for the next ten years to 'tackle low aspirations in early years, schools, colleges and other services' (2007). The 'Children's' Plan' reinforces the need to involve parents in education in order to secure greater well-being of young people, and also to secure higher achievement.

At the core of the 'Children's Plan' is the firm belief that parental engagement makes a significant difference to educational outcomes and that parents and carers[1] have a key role to play in raising educational standards. In summary, the more engaged parents are in their children's learning, the more likely their children are to achieve academic success.

Parental engagement makes a significant difference to the educational outcomes of young people, and parents therefore have a key role to play in raising educational standards. The more engaged parents are in the education of their children, the more likely their children are to succeed in the education system. Both the school improvement and school effectiveness research consistently show that parental engagement is one of the key factors in securing higher student achievement. Highly effective schools are schools with a high degree of community involvement and parental support.

Schools that improve and sustain improvement almost always have engaged the community and have built strong links with parents. The key to success resides in teachers, parents and students seeing parental engagement as critical for academic success. Where schools have built positive relationships with parents and have actively worked to embrace racial, religious, and language differences, evidence of sustained school improvement can be found.

Contemporary findings also show that schools that have ameliorated some of the more negative aspects of social deprivation, have succeeded in linking with the community and constructing an environment where learning is encouraged and endorsed (Harris et al. 2006). These schools succeed because they have deliberately and purposefully embraced the parental community to develop a shared learning culture.

Developing and sustaining effective partnerships between the home, the community and the school is, without question, the most important component of successful school improvement (Harris and Goodall 2008). When such partnerships are developed and sustained, children in all settings, but particularly high poverty contexts, learn far more effectively. While engaging parents in schooling in highly disadvantaged communities is not without its difficulties, where this is achieved the benefits to young people can be significant (Harris and Goodall 2006).

---

[1] The term 'parents' is used to include those adults caring for children, i.e. who have the direct responsibility for the safety and well-being of young people.

Epstein et al. (2002) suggest that there are *six critical practices* that schools can use to enrich parents/community partnerships:

- Assist families with parenting skills
- Improve communication with families
- Increase volunteer opportunities with families
- Increase family engagement in student learning in the home
- Involve families in school decision-making
- Increase collaboration with the community.

As the case study examples in this book illustrate, these six practices can be highly effective in securing better relationships with parents and productive two-way communication between parents and the school. Overall, there seem to be significant improvements in parent-school relationships where there is outreach work with parents, parent education programmes, resources for parents to support learning in the home and clear two-way communication.

It is important, however, that school communication with parents should not simply focus on student problems or behavioural issues. Communication should also reinforce and highlight student successes and help families to help their children to be more effective learners. It should help teachers and parents to understand student problems and potential difficulties and upheavals wherever they occur, in the home, classroom or wider community. For parents with a home language other than English, efforts should be made to translate some information into their language.

Time to engage?

One of the most cited reasons for parents not being involved in schooling is work commitments. Lack of time and childcare difficulties can be significant barriers, particularly for those parents who are working full time. Working parents are unlikely to be able to attend events held in the day or at the end of school. Single parents are also restricted in this respect and can find attending school events difficult. This issue of time, however, is only part of a larger and more complex socio-economic picture.

Certain parents can be very resistant to the school and actively avoid contact. These parents have considerable difficulties in their exchanges with teachers and school administration. Many have had a negative experience of schooling and therefore remain resistant or even hostile to any form of engagement. Parents evenings can create parental frustration and confusion. Some parents can feel intimidated or even patronized at such events even though schools make every effort to be welcoming. Whilst there is a broadly held desire amongst most parents to support their children's learning, there are material and psychological barriers that operate differentially and discriminatingly across different parental groups (Harris and Goodall 2007).

One way forward is for schools to think about holding events off site, at different times of the day, rather than a blocked time at the school. As we will see later, effective use of ICT can also alleviate the pressure of face-to-face communication as parents can access information about their child's progress 24/7 and can locate resources to assist with learning in the home.

The attribution of responsibility for education is a key factor in shaping parents' views about what they feel is important or necessary or even permissible for them to do. Role definitions are shaped by family and cultural experiences and are subject to potential internal conflict, e.g. parent as housekeeper or breadwinner or nurse or teacher. Parents will be involved if they see that supporting and enhancing their child's school achievement is part of their 'job' as a parent. Likewise, parents will get involved if they feel they have the capacity to contribute.

Effective two-way communication is essential if a comprehensive partnership between school and home is to be maintained. To foster effective communication with families, there are a number of actions that can foster an atmosphere of trust. These include:

- being open, helpful, friendly and respectful to all families
- communicating clearly and frequently about policies, programs and student progress
- encouraging family feedback
- allowing parents to bring another adult to key events such as parents evenings
- providing one point of call for parents so that they are clear whom they can talk to
- using ICT to offer other forms of communication and access to information
- providing informal activities at which parents, staff and community members can interact.

Schools that have succeeded in improving their performance are also schools where teaching and learning are given the highest priority and where the relationships with the local community are positive. Effective schools partner with families and build two-way communication. They do not rely on external interventions and programmes, but develop strong local and community relationships. They are also schools that provide a wide variety of services, particularly in those communities facing the greatest challenges.

Student voice

In securing stronger partnerships between home and the community, students have a significant contribution to make, not as passive objects but as active players. School improvement is secured by changing the patterns of relationships between parents, staff and students. Despite hundreds of studies of parental engagement and school improvement, there have until recently been relatively few studies that have focused on students' contribution to engaging parents in their learning.

The emerging evidence base now shows the contribution that students can make to gain a better understanding of the reasons why parents engage or do not engage with schools. Writers like Rudduck et al. (2003) have long argued that students not only have a great deal to say about their experiences of learning, but that, also, their voices are constructive and informative and can help schools to build strong partnerships with the community. Where opportunities are made for students to become active participants in the process of securing parental engagement, the gains appear to be significant.

A recent study has demonstrated the potential of involving students in reaching out to the community. This study focused particularly on engaging 'hard-to-reach parents' in a disadvantaged community (Harris et al. 2008). The research spanned a full year and took place in three phases. The first phase involved initial school visits and the identification of a group of students and a group of lunchtime supervisors who would be the researchers on the project. In phase two, university researchers met with lunchtime supervisors to get their perspectives, as parents and members of the community, on the various issues relating to the engagement of parents.

During the third phase, a group of Year 8 students from each secondary school in the project were trained as researchers to collect data from other students. The student researchers collected data from a cross section of Year 6 students in their feeder primary schools. The questions focused on the students' perspectives on parental engagement and tried to identify some of the barriers to engagement. The student data was subsequently analysed and coded.

In addition, a group of support staff, including lunchtime supervisors, were trained as researchers and contributed to a DVD about data gathering from parents. This group subsequently interviewed hard-to-reach parents in the community. The project concluded that where students are co-researchers and contribute to the process of engaging other students in dialogue about engaging parents, the potential for improving practice is greatly enhanced.

While it takes time and considerable preparation to build a climate in which teachers, support staff and students feel comfortable working together on issues of parental engagement, the benefits can be substantial. However, role boundaries have to be crossed and the limits of trust have to be tested. Rudduck (2001: 14) suggests that there are four levels of student voice:

- Listening to students – where students are a source of data; teachers respond to student data but students are not involved in discussion of data; there is no feedback; teachers act on the data.
- Students as active participants – where teachers initiate enquiry and interpret the data but students take some role in decision-making.
- Students as researchers – where students are involved in enquiry and have an active role in decision-making.
- Students as fully active researchers and co-researchers – where students and teachers jointly initiate enquiry; students play an active role in decision-making together with teachers, they jointly plan action in the light of data and review the impact of the intervention.

Where students are fully active researchers and co-researchers, it can have a two-fold effect. First, it puts the issue of parental engagement in learning at the forefront of their thinking, thus creating a better understanding. Secondly, it encourages them to help the school find solutions and more effective ways of communicating with parents.

Effective parental engagement

There are literally hundreds of books, journal articles and reports on the subject of parental engagement and while a great many of these publications are informative and useful they do not help schools to engage parents more effectively. It is clear that there is a great variety of practice, some effective, some less so, including telephone and written communications, attending school functions, parents serving as classroom volunteers, parent-teacher conferences, homework/tutoring assistance, parents as governors and real time reporting. If the aspiration of engaging parents in student learning is to be achieved, we have to think differently about the forms of parental engagement that schools implement.

There is no particular amalgam of practices that work more effectively than others, but it is clear that gains in learning can only be achieved if there is a *direct link* between parental engagement and learning. There are three ways to think about this relationship:

- Parental engagement *for* learning
- Parental engagement *through* learning
- Parental engagement *about* learning.

Parental engagement *for* learning occurs when schools take specific steps to connect parents to classroom learning through materials, online support or face-to-face instruction. Parental engagement *through* learning occurs via parental study groups or parent education classes held by the school. Parental engagement *about* learning is where parents actively engage with teachers and students to understand more about the process of learning and are made aware of the range of meta-cognitive strategies that can improve learning outcomes.

In order to maximise parental engagement *for, through and about* learning, six essential elements need to be promoted:

1 **Communication** between home and school has to be regular, two-way, and meaningful. Effective communication requires school-initiated contact with the parent and parent-initiated contact with the school where both parties provide vital information about a child's strengths, challenges and accomplishments. To communicate effectively, both parties must be aware of, and address, issues such as cultural diversity, language differences and special needs.

2 **Responsible parenting** is promoted and supported. The family plays a key role in a child's educational environment. Schools can support positive parenting by respecting and affirming the strengths and skills needed by parents to fulfil their role.

3 **Parents play an integral role in assisting student learning.** Student achievement increases when parents are actively involved in the learning process. Schools need to provide opportunities for parents

to learn the most effective ways of supporting their child's educational needs. This includes information about how parents can support certain student behaviours, e.g. punctuality and regular attendance, that are closely tied to student success in school.

4   Parents are welcomed as **volunteers** in schools. Parent volunteers can obtain a better understanding of learning processes. Therefore, parents should be encouraged to volunteer at all educational levels.

5.   Parents should be full partners in the **decisions** that affect their children. Schools need to actively enlist parent participation in decision-making. Efforts should be made to recruit and support the participation of parents representing diverse student groups. The role of parents in decision-making needs to be continually evaluated, refined, and expanded at the school level.

6.   Parents, school and community need to **collaborate** in order to enhance student learning, strengthen families and improve schools. Parents, educators and community members need to work together in order to promote and effectively increase educational opportunities for children. Providing all students with equal access to quality education is a primary goal. It is vital that all partners (parents, educators, businesses and communities) have the opportunity to provide input and offer resources to meet this goal. Developing cooperative efforts and providing access to resources will ensure improved academic achievement for all students, as well as better quality educational processes.

Some studies suggest that parental engagement can reinforce the existing power divisions between schools, teachers and parents, and can reproduce, rather than break down, existing educational inequalities around class, gender and ethnicity. This is, in part, because parental engagement initiatives presuppose that schools, parents and students are equally willing to, and capable of, developing parental engagement schemes, which is not always the case.

Summary

Parents, carers and family members are by far the most important influences on their children's lives. They influence how young people think about education, their future and society. Therefore, their support for schools and engagement in learning is crucial if improving learning outcomes for *each* student in *each* setting is to be more than an aspiration.

Questions

- How are parents engaged in learning in your school? Are these approaches effective?
- What other approaches could you explore to engage parents in learning?
- What help or support do you need?

Parental engagement and student achievement 2

The evidence is convincing; families have a major influence on children's achievement in school and through life. When schools, families and community groups work together to support learning, children tend to do better in school, stay in school longer, and like school more.

(Henderson and Mapp 2002: 16)

Introduction

The evidence concerning parental engagement is both consistent and conclusive. It shows that parental engagement makes a *significant* difference to learning outcomes. Inevitably, research concerning the impact of parental engagement upon achievement and attainment is complex due to the interaction and influence of many factors and variables. However, the contemporary evidence points towards a powerful association between parental engagement and student achievement. It also acknowledges that parental engagement is only one of many factors that influences educational achievement, but highlights that its influence is particularly powerful (Fan and Chen 2001).

Disentangling the web of variables enmeshing the whole of family-school relationships and their impact on learning is a complex task. But it is clear that levels of engagement vary considerably depending on the parents and the context in which they find themselves. As highlighted earlier, a major factor affecting parental engagement in learning is SES (socio-economic status), whether indexed by occupational class or parental (especially maternal) level of education. Study after study has shown that SES mediates both parental engagement and student achievement.

Many parents from some ethnic groupings know little about the education system. These parents are often seen as indifferent or difficult or 'hard to reach'. Yet, for many of these parents the school itself is inaccessible and hard to reach. The ethnic diversity among parents is a major challenge for many schools, particularly those with high immigrant populations where language and culture can both be barriers to effective home/school communication. Such barriers, if they are not adequately addressed, can contribute to widening the gap between the involved and the uninvolved parents and the gap between achievers and the underachievers.

What is parental engagement?

Parental engagement can be defined in a variety of ways. It can include the idea of parental involvement and, indeed, the terms *engagement* and *involvement* are often used interchangeably even though they mean different things. Parents can be *involved* in school activities without being *engaged* in their children's learning. Yet it is parental engagement in learning that brings significant gains in achievement.

Involvement means parents coming into school either informally (for example to bring children into school or to provide some information for the school) or formally (for example, for parents evening, meetings or adult learning classes). Parental engagement occurs where parents are *actively* involved in supporting learning *in the home* through extension or support activities, homework or online activities. The concept of parental engagement essentially encompasses all parental activities that directly support children's learning.

Parental engagement has been defined as representing many different parental behaviours and parenting practices. These include:

- parental aspirations for their children's academic achievement and their conveyance of such aspirations to their children
- parents' communication with children about school, parents' participation in school activities
- parents' communication with teachers about their children
- parental rules imposed at home that are considered to be education-related.

This range of interpretations suggests that parental engagement is multifaceted in nature, because parental engagement subsumes a wide variety of parental behavioural patterns and parenting practices.

Epstein (1992) recognizes six different types of parental engagement:

(1) Parent practices that establish a **positive learning environment at home**.
(2) **Parent-school communications** about school programs and student progress.
(3) **Parent participation** and volunteering at school.
(4) Parent and school communications regarding **learning activities at home**.
(5) Parent engagement in **school decision-making** and governance.
(6) Parent access to **community resources** that increase students' learning opportunities.

While all of these are important, it is the *first* of these that makes a difference to student learning and achievement.

In a modern, changing society, the traditional definitions of 'parent' and 'family' are no longer appropriate. Such definitions exclude single parents and guardians, and do not cater for 'looked-after children'. Schools are required by law to have a wide range of dealings with students' parents. The question 'who are a student's parents?' is, however, not always as straightforward as it sounds. Additionally, schools can sometimes find themselves caught up in disputes between a number of adults, each claiming to have parental responsibility for a child.

Section 576 of the Education Act 1996 defines parent as:

- all natural (biological) parents, whether they are married or not
- any person who, although not a natural parent, has parental responsibility for a child or young person
- any person who, although not a natural parent, has care of a child or young person.

Having parental responsibility means assuming all the rights, duties, powers, responsibilities and authority that a parent of a child has by law. People other than a child's natural parents can acquire parental responsibility through:

- being granted a residence order
- being appointed a guardian
- being named in an emergency protection order (although parental

responsibility in such a case is limited to taking reasonable steps to safeguard or promote the child's welfare)
- adopting a child.

In addition, a local authority can acquire parental responsibility if it is named in the care order for a child. Everyone who is a parent, whether they are a resident or non-resident parent, has the same right to participate in decisions about a child's education and receive information about the child. However, for day-to-day purposes, the school's main contact is likely to be the parent with whom the child lives on school days.

School and LA staff must treat all parents equally, unless there is a court order limiting an individual's exercise of parental responsibility. Individuals who have parental responsibility for, or care of, a child have the same rights as natural parents, for example:

- to receive information, e.g. student reports
- to participate in activities, e.g. vote in elections for parent governors
- to be asked to give consent, e.g. to the child taking part in school trips
- to be informed about meetings involving the child, e.g. a governors' meeting on the child's exclusion.

The welfare of a child is of paramount consideration for all schools. However, where a parent's action or proposed action conflicts with the school's ability to act in the child's best interests, the school staff should try to resolve the problem with that parent but should avoid becoming involved in the conflict.

While issues of definition are not as important as the action to support young people and their learning, it is clear that there is a danger that certain young people may be marginalized because their family circumstances do not fit the conventional model. Schools can be inherently conservative places and therefore it is important that every effort is made to engage adults who have direct responsibility for the well-being and safety of young people. Many schools are already doing this very well and are benefiting from the additional support that such engagement brings.

Impact and effect of parental engagement

Parental engagement has a significant effect on children's achievement and adjustment even after all other factors (such as social class, maternal education and poverty) have been taken out of the equation. This effect is bigger than that of schooling itself. Parents' support for learning in the home is far more important to their achievement than their social class or the level of education.

From an extensive and comprehensive overview of the research evidence,[2] one overarching conclusion has emerged: taken as a whole, there is a *positive and convincing relationship* between family involvement and benefits for students, including improved academic achievement. This relationship holds across families of *all* economic, racial, ethnic, and educational backgrounds and for students at *all* ages. Although there is less research on the effects of community involvement, it also suggests benefits for schools, families, and students, including improved achievement and behaviour.

The direct benefits of parental engagement for students include:

- higher academic performance (in standardized tests or exams)
- better attendance
- improved behaviour at home and at school
- better social skills and adaptation to school.

It is important to point out that it takes more than engaged parents to produce high student achievement. Many studies of high-performing schools identify several key characteristics associated with improvement. These include high standards and expectations for all students and curriculum, as well as effective instruction and assessments aligned with those standards. They also include effective leadership, frequent monitoring of teaching and learning, focused professional development and high levels of parent and community involvement. It is the particular amalgam of these factors that produces high achievement.

Parental engagement is necessary but not sufficient to raise achievement in schools. However, it is the most powerful improvement lever we have and in many schools still the most under-utilized way of raising school performance. So what needs to happen?

One way forward is to have dedicated programmes aimed at

[2] Henderson, A. and Mapp, K. (2002), *A New Wave of Evidence: The Impact of School, Family and Community Connections on Student Achievement.* Austin, TX: Southwest Educational Development Laboratory.

engaging parents from the beginning of their child's education. Early childhood and pre-school programmes such as 'Sure-Start', which prepare parents to work with their children on learning at home, have significant, positive effects on achievement and behaviour. Children's attainment tends to improve the longer they are in the program, and evidence suggests that they make greater gains than children not in the programmes.

The studies that compared levels of involvement, found that achievement was directly related to the extent to which parents were engaged in the programme. Children from all family backgrounds and income levels made gains and in some cases the children having the most difficulty in school made the greatest gains. It would seem that the continuity of family involvement at home is important, i.e. the longer parents are engaged with their child's learning, the greater the gains. The more families support their children's learning and educational progress, the more their children tend to do well in school and the more likely they are to continue their education. Yet, it is not only younger children who benefit from such programmes, older children benefit as well.

As the case studies in this book illustrate, there are a wealth of ways in which parents can support learning at secondary school level and can obtain real-time information about their child's progress and academic performance. In the transition from primary to secondary school, the evidence shows that joint parent and school support can have a significant impact on students' sense of confidence and well-being. Students reported three major ways in which their transition to secondary was assisted:

1. **Support from parents**. Parents talking to students about school, checking homework, attending events, and volunteering at school.
2. **Support from teachers**. Teachers taking time to help students and being supportive rather than critical.
3. **Support from the school**. Students feeling accepted, respected, and included at school. Feeling like they belong.

Students reporting high parent engagement and a high sense of belonging, or high parent engagement and high teacher support, performed much better at secondary school in the initial phase of transition than students who reported low support at any one of the three levels. This suggests very strongly that if children don't feel connected to school in some way, and don't have the support of their parents, this transition phase is more difficult and there may be negative outcomes in terms of learning and progression.

Engaging all parents?

When students report feeling support from both home and school, they tend to also do better in school. They say that they have more self-confidence and feel school is more important. They are also less disruptive, gain higher test scores, and are more likely to go on to further education. For many children, home and school are two very different worlds. But if there can be some congruence of support from parents, school and teachers, then students are more likely to see the benefits of learning. However, the challenge for many schools is exactly how to engage *all* parents.

It is clear that many parents are not willing to engage with schools and/or lack the self efficacy to feel that they have anything to contribute. Evidence shows that parents' sense of their self efficacy influences how engaged they are in primary and secondary school. Parents who have a high sense of efficacy believe they can:

- help their children do well in school
- help their children to be happy, and be safe
- overcome negative influences
- keep their children away from troublemakers, illegal drugs or alcohol
- have a positive impact on their children's learning and achievement.

Generally, the greater parents' sense of self efficacy, the more closely they tend to be involved with school. Also, the higher parents' feelings of self efficacy, the more their children reported doing better in school and feeling happy, safe, and stable. Families who live in safe, higher-income areas tend to have a higher sense of efficacy than families living in areas of disadvantage. So it is fairly predictable that families living in high poverty are those that find it more difficult to engage with the school and to positively influence learning in the home.

The impact of parental engagement on learning is considerable, but for certain families its impact is far greater. For families in more disadvantaged settings, the net result of engaging parents in learning can have a far greater impact on learning than engaging families in more affluent settings. Put bluntly, if the parenting engagement practices of most working class parents could be raised to the levels of the best working class parents, very significant advances in achievement might reasonably be expected (Desforges and Abouchaar 2003; Fan and Chen 2001).

Among the non-school factors of school achievement (e.g. socio-economic background, parent's educational attainment, family structure, ethnicity and parental engagement) it is parental engagement that is the most strongly connected to attainment. Parents' aspiration or expectations have a strong impact on their children's subsequent results at school, while the effect of supervision of homework is only marginal.

Differences between parents in their level of engagement can be associated with the way parents feel about school and teachers. Some parents are put off by school and can feel anxiety about being 'put down' by teachers. Middle class parents use the vocabulary of teachers, feel entitled to treat teachers as equals and have access to childcare and transportation. This allows them to construct their relationships with the school with more comfort and trust. Other parents from different social groups can feel less confident and secure about talking to teachers. They can feel intimidated and shy. The key issue is, how do schools engage these parents, how do schools view these parents and how do schools ensure that those parents with the most social capital are not the only voices heard?

Schools in challenging circumstances

Schools in challenging circumstances face multiple problems. They are most likely to have higher than average numbers of students with low literacy levels on entry. They are also likely to have a higher proportion of refugee children or students that have been excluded from other schools. Incidents of violence, crime and drugs also tend to be more prevalent in communities where poverty and disadvantage are endemic. These powerful, interlocking variables make the daily business of educating young people demanding and often dangerous for teachers.

Schools located in areas of high socio-economic deprivation are more likely to be populated with students typically categorized as 'disadvantaged' or 'at risk'. They generally face a greater risk of school failure by comparison to their more affluent counterparts and have significantly lower levels of social and cultural capital. In addition, with disadvantage comes diversity and the more severe the disadvantage the greater the diversity within the student population.

Within any community, parents' expectations set the frame within which young people develop, shape their own expectations and make decisions. However, as we have highlighted, there are significant differences between parents in their level of engagement that are clearly associated with social class, poverty, health, and also with parental perception of their role and their levels of confidence in fulfilling it. Students from families with low socio-economic indicators are more likely to be disaffected from school, as are students who attend schools that have a high percentage of students of low socio-economic status.

As these risk factors compound, students from low socio-economic status families are even more likely to be dissatisfied with school. This phenomenon of 'double jeopardy' is also evident in analyses of student achievement: low SES students who also attend schools that predominantly serve low socio-economic status students are especially at risk of poor school performance because they have two factors working together.

Students are more likely to be engaged in learning if they attend schools that have a higher than average socio-economic status, a strong disciplinary climate, good student-teacher relations and high expectations. Students from low SES families are more likely to attend schools where the average socio-economic status is low. This is not to suggest that all young people from low SES backgrounds are likely to underachieve or to become disaffected, but to highlight the challenges these young people and their families face in overcoming some of the cultural, social and financial barriers that stand in the way of reaching their full potential.

Differences relating to economic status are strongly related to parental engagement. While parents want the best for their children, working class parents may not automatically expect the same outcomes as middle class parents (National Centre for Social Research 2006). As Lupton (2006) points out, 'most working class parents think education is important but they see it as something that happens in the school, not the home.' Their expectations of social mobility through education also remain small and therefore the potential to break out of their circumstances becomes much harder.

In a growing number of areas, community groups are representing parents and residents in low-income communities. These groups include the larger community of business leaders and public officials, and endeavour to build public support for changes in education policy. The goal of these efforts is to improve outcomes for all students through increased funding and educational resources. In low-income urban and rural areas, many schools are underfunded, overcrowded, and poor-performing. Schools in these areas are more likely to have crumbling facilities and poor learning environments. Therefore, the community voice is one that is important for parents and young people alike.

A lack of social and political capital can seriously restrict families' capacity to support their children's learning and make sure they get a high-quality education. When parents feel they have the power to change and control their circumstances, children tend to do better in school. Their parents are also better equipped to help them. When schools work with families to develop their connections, families become powerful allies of the schools and advocates for public education.

Building social and political capital in the school requires parents and teachers to use the same vocabulary. It necessitates shared rules of behaviour, and the resources to make these connections possible, such as transportation and childcare. There are some obvious ways in which schools and parents can connect most effectively, particularly in the most challenging areas:

- Ask families about the best times for them to attend events at school.
- Ask what kind of events they would like to attend.
- Ask what they think would make the school better.
- Promote families' connections with each other, with teachers and other school staff, and with community groups.
- Translate all communications with families into their home languages and provide an interpreter at meetings.
- Offer childcare, meals, and transportation for major activities at school.

Not all parents want to be involved in schools, not all parents are interested in their children's learning. Some schools see parents as a nuisance and try and minimize their involvement, some schools see parental engagement as interference. On both sides of the fence there can be misunderstanding, suspicion and apathy. The challenge is to break down these barriers as the gains on both sides are too significant to lose.

Any attempt to form genuine collaborations among school staff, parents, and community members must start with building relationships of respect. The building of relationships must be intentional and consistent. When outreach efforts reflect a sincere desire to engage parents and community members as partners in children's education, the studies show that they respond positively. Increasingly, the communities served by schools are diverse in terms of class, ethnicity and culture.

Evidence suggests that educators should make every attempt to learn about the concerns of the families and how they define and perceive their role in the school. If parents don't attend activities arranged by school staff and held at the school, the school should not assume that 'parents don't care'. Instead, school could explore other avenues that better reflect the communities' priorities. Parents and community members tend to feel respected when schools genuinely attempt to understand and relate to their needs.

But who engages?

Evidence would suggest that in the majority of cases it is the mother who takes the lead in communicating with the school and supporting learning activities in the home. This is particularly true for mothers of primary school children, where there is a need to take and collect children to school. This affords more informal conversation with other parents and teachers on a regular basis.

A recent telephone survey, which involved 2019 households, established that 29 per cent of parents felt very engaged in school, more so in primary than in secondary schools. The survey showed that mothers felt more involved than fathers. Of the sample, 35 per cent strongly agreed that they wanted to be more involved in their children's learning, while around 75 per cent of parents wanted to be at least 'somewhat more' involved. Within the survey, 94 per cent found the school 'welcoming' and 84 per cent reported that the school was willing to involve them. Despite this level of satisfaction, 16 per cent felt they might be seen as troublemakers if they talked too much. While many parents wanted to increase their engagement to include, for example, supporting extra-curricular initiatives, they felt that the main barriers to further engagement were the limitations of their own time.

The vast majority of the parents and carers said they felt very or fairly involved in their child's education, but this engagement varied across different groups. A lower level of engagement was claimed by men. They have fewer opportunities to go to parents' evenings, help with fund-raising activities, help with dinner duties and school trips and help out in class. Men are also less likely to help with their child's homework because of work patterns. Those men in social class D and E (i.e. those from households where the chief income earner's occupation is an unskilled manual job or where the family is dependent on state benefits only) are less likely to be involved in their children's education.

Recent findings show that men, and those mothers working full-time, saw work commitments as the main barrier to engagement. Men aged under 35 and women under 35 were the most likely to say the demands of childcare prevented them from being engaged with the school. Slightly less predictably, those aged 45 plus, those in social class D and E, and those for whom English was not their first language, tended to say there were no specific barriers. However, the evidence suggests that these parents are less likely to involve themselves in education than their younger counterparts. Across all groups, students do better if their parents helped them see the importance of their school work.

In terms of race, parental engagement can became a significant discriminating factor between groups. Successful Afro-Americans were found to have levels of parental engagement that were equal to, or higher than, those of successful Euro-Americans and significantly higher than those of unsuccessful Afro-American students. Drawing on a study of 10,000 high school students, it was concluded:

> Parents who are more involved in their adolescents' schooling, regardless of parents' gender or educational level, have offspring who do better in school, irrespective of the child's gender, ethnicity or family structure.
>
> (Bogenschneider (1999), in C. Desforges & A. Abouchaar (2003): 729)

All studies report that most parents are keen for their youngsters to 'do well'. In summary, the general impact of parental engagement seems to work in support of student attainment across all ethnic groups. Parental engagement, especially in the form of parental values and aspirations modelled in the home, is a major force shaping students' achievement and adjustment.

So how do we engage parents and why are some parents engaged more than others?

How to engage parents

While the effects of home environments on school learning are significant and well documented in the research literature, evidence that learning can be enhanced by school-based initiatives to influence family behaviours is much more limited. This may be because parent engagement programs tend to be small in scope and not focused on student learning, and primarily inclusive only of parents who choose to participate in activities at the school. From the limited evidence available, successful school efforts to engage families include the following:

- Building a foundation of trust and respect
- Connecting parent-engagement strategies to learning objectives
- Reaching out to engage parents beyond the school.

These features have been typically found in schools where parent engagement is measurably high, in specific programs that demonstrate positive effects on learning outcomes, and in schools that exhibit high levels of achievement (Henderson and Mapp 2002). Effective parent engagement must be comprehensive in nature, with the school consistently interfacing with parents at many points, in many venues, over the course of the schooling years.

The school may affect home environments in positive ways through intentional, consistent interaction with parents. Relationships among students, families, and school personnel can exert an influence on family behaviours that in turn are positively linked to school learning. As teachers enlist the support of parents in learning, in different ways at different points in time, the child's learning increasingly becomes the focus of their interactions with parents.

The increasing effects of more frequent and higher quality interactions among teachers and parents engender trust and respect, increased social capital for children, and a school community more supportive of each child's school success. Evidence has shown that community-based organizations and schools are most effective in engaging families in their children's education if their efforts are comprehensive, focused, and coherent.

There are a number of things that schools can do to increase parental engagement:

1. Schools can clearly articulate their expectations of parents.
2. They can regularly communicate with parents about what children are learning, suggesting what parents can do to help.
3. Schools can establish school-home agreements, reading school-home links and explicit homework policies that outline expectations and support for children's learning.
4. Schools can provide opportunities for parents to talk with school personnel about parents' role in their children's education through home visits, family nights, and well-planned parent-teacher conferences and open houses.
5. Schools can provide education for parents to better help their children meet state learning standards.

Finally, an ongoing conversation between parents and teachers about the role of each in *learning* is central to building the relationship and understanding that enhances school performance.

This type of engagement is often led by parents and community members. Strategies of community organising are different from traditional parent involvement and are openly focused on building families' power and political skills to hold schools accountable. A new group of studies found that community organising contributed the following changes:

- Better school facilities
- Improved school leadership and staffing
- Higher-quality learning programs for students
- New resources and programs to improve teaching and curriculum
- New funding for after-school programs and family supports.

When programs and initiatives focus on building respectful and trusting relationships among school staff, families, and community members, they are effective in creating and sustaining family and community connections with schools. It is clear that relationships matter, and how parents and community members are viewed and treated by school staff as assets to the process of raising student achievement rather than liabilities, is the key to promoting effective learning. Staff-to-staff and staff-to-parent relationships at a school can hugely influence the quality of learning and support for learning. Effective programmes to engage families and community embrace a philosophy of partnership. The responsibility for children's educational development is a collaborative enterprise among parents, school staff, and community members.

Parents' roles and engagement in schools have been understood largely in terms of 'what they do' and how that fits or does not fit with the needs of the child or the goals of the school. This approach to parental engagement relies on the school dictating the terms. Many parents find this difficult. In many schools there are few choices about the way in which parents engage. Parents are expected to participate in school-sanctioned ways or, by implication, their children's educational growth may suffer.

There are many more school-initiated 'parental' programmes or projects than initiatives that have included parents as equal partners and decision makers. Parents often have rich networks and resources that could be drawn upon by the school. They may have ideas about the forms of engagement they would enjoy or could relate to. They just need to be equal partners in the design of activities and programmes for them to be most effective. Schools need to take some risks and let parents take the lead but clearly provide input and direction.

Summary

So what does the evidence tell us? Essentially, it confirms the long held view that what parents *do with their children at home* through the age ranges is much more significant than any other factor open to educational influence. Parent engagement in school education has been shown to foster positive learning outcomes. Schools that succeed in engaging families from very diverse backgrounds share two key practices:

- Building trusting collaborative relationships among teachers, families, and community members
- Recognizing, respecting and addressing families' needs, as well as class and cultural difference.

Some of the more critical literature in the area has indicated how polices concerning parental engagement are fraught with problems. It has been suggested that it is a way for the State to abdicate its responsibilities. Other writers have indicated how it has become fashionable to promote the idea of community engagement within the context of 'active democratic citizenship', especially in a scenario characterized by attempts to cut back on public spending.

So what do we know?

- We know that *parental engagement* is a critical part of high quality education, a safe and disciplined learning environment, and student achievement.
- We know that what the family *does* is more important than what the family income or education level is.
- We are clear that *all parents* want the best education for their children, most parents want to be more engaged in their child's education, but many don't know how to become involved.
- We know that *most teachers* feel that parent engagement is a vital part of student achievement, but many of them do not know how to get the parents engaged.

So what needs to happen? Schools need to look critically at their current ways of engaging parents and to seek additional or alternative practices that encourage parents to participate in learning. Schools also need to encourage parents to become partners in learning.

The next chapter outlines the work of the 'Engaging Parents Raising Achievement' campaign, which was designed to create stronger parental engagement in learning. It focuses on what needs to happen for parental engagement to impact on student achievement.

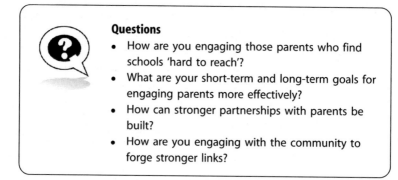

Questions
- How are you engaging those parents who find schools 'hard to reach'?
- What are your short-term and long-term goals for engaging parents more effectively?
- How can stronger partnerships with parents be built?
- How are you engaging with the community to forge stronger links?

Engaging parents to raise achievement 3

Introduction

This chapter outlines the scope and nature of the 'Engaging Parents to Raise Achievement' (EPRA) campaign, which was designed to support schools in a range of development work aimed at securing more effective parental engagement. The project aimed to highlight the important relationship between parental engagement and student learning and to generate innovative practice.

The campaign encouraged schools to explore two routes. First, to look at their *traditional practice* with parents and consider how this work could be developed or extended. Secondly, schools were encouraged to *innovate* and to *trial* different approaches to parental engagement that would impact positively upon the quality of student learning. Student achievement and learning were placed at the core of the EPRA agenda and schools were encouraged to develop or extend their practices under four strands:

- **Supporting parents to help their children learn** – aimed to enable schools to equip parents with the knowledge and skills to support their children's learning from home. This included encouraging schools to focus on activities to help parents understand elements of the curriculum, advice about revision techniques at KS 3 and 4 as well as more diverse activities designed to stimulate parental engagement with schools and raise parents' aspirations for their children.
- **Personalizing provision for parents as learners** – aimed to build on evidence that parents' own achievement and experience of the education system is a key determinant of their expectations for their children's learning. This strand aimed to enable schools to re-engage

parents with low or no formal skills or qualifications in learning. By breaking down barriers between the school and the parent, and igniting an interest in learning, the aim of this work was to shift negative attitudes to education held by some parents, which may contribute to generational under-achievement in some groups.

- **iReporting** strand was designed to encourage schools to push the boundaries of practice by using new technologies to engage parents in their children's learning. Schools were encouraged to explore the most effective means of using new technologies to keep parents up to date with their children's studies, to update them about progress and to look at forms of effective intervention. This strand also encouraged schools to look at solutions for parents without access to a computer, and to explore innovative approaches to providing up-to-date 24/7 data through traditional methods of reporting and information sharing.

- **Enhancing pastoral care** strand encouraged schools to develop support for parents in their interactions with the school and with their child. Its aim was to enable schools to engage parents usually missed in broader parental engagement programmes. For example, fathers, Somali and Bengali parents and the most disengaged white families from areas of high deprivation. This strand encouraged schools to look at strategies and approaches to improve parenting in the home through the use of dedicated staff such as School Home Support Workers and Parent Support Advisers.

At the launch of EPRA, schools that were identified as *progressive* in developing 'traditional' or 'new' practice in engaging parents, shared their development work with other schools. This show-case was intended to help other schools move their practice forward. For example, The Compton School in Barnet shared an *audit tool* they had used to review their existing practice with parents. This tool covered a range of practices: information-sharing, communication, joining in, reporting and involvement activity. Another school, Sharnbrook Upper School, Bucking-hamshire, shared how their *vertical tutoring system* enabled staff to have the time to be a single point of contact for a smaller number of parents. In comparison to the traditional tutor group system with 30 students per tutor, the new system involved all staff (teaching and support) being responsible for groups of 10 to 15 students.

Cardinal Wiseman School in Birmingham shared their *online reporting system* and the processes by which they had developed this to be user friendly and meaningful to staff, parents and students. All the schools shared how they had worked to empower parents to work more effectively with their children and to promote learning in the home.

The EPRA campaign was intrinsically *school led* in its philosophy and its approach. It replicated the methodology of the 'Raising Achievement Transforming Learning Project' (RATL) in the respect that at its core was the belief that solutions to challenges faced by schools reside within schools and the profession. The RATL methodology *challenges* schools and professionals to think that anything is possible; it *motivates* by showing how schools have found solutions and it *inspires* by demonstrating that solutions lead to such positive outcomes for students.

The 'challenge, motivation and inspiration' for the EPRA campaign came from schools that were already making progress with parental engagement; schools that recognized that parents were an underutilized resource for raising achievement; schools that saw the challenges to effective engagement were surmountable and were committed to working together to find solutions.

The key to the success of the campaign rested on schools *sharing* their learning. To facilitate and encourage this shared learning, the 103 schools that were part of the EPRA campaign recorded, collated, evaluated and disseminated their activities through the academic year. The process of sharing their work created a common view across the EPRA schools that anything was possible; that ideas could be taken from one school, adapted and developed to suit the context of another and further developed through professional dialogue and support.

Crossley and Corbyn (2006) compare 'school-led system leadership' approaches with 'top down, policy led' attempts at change. Asserting why school-led models work, they highlight the value school leaders place on learning *from and with* their peers. They argue that school-based approaches remove the opportunity for the excuse 'it won't work with these kids and these parents' when it is proved to work in another school with the same intake and parent profile.

The creation of empowering 'can do' networks of schools and professionals meant that it was possible to find solutions, develop further practice, and to demonstrate a positive impact on student outcomes. The EPRA network has enabled schools to focus on what works and what is possible, and to adapt solutions to suit *the particular school* context and need.

Schools in the EPRA campaign trialled a wide range of new

and innovative approaches to engaging parents in learning. They also adapted and developed existing practices. Through extending and developing their work with parents, the EPRA schools no longer viewed parental contact as being confined to 9 a.m. to 3 p.m. Similarly, they tended not to take a 'one size fits all' approach to parental engagement.

Through sustained shared professional learning and dialogue, EPRA schools developed models of parental engagement that are personalized and effective. The schools embrace the ethos of the 'Every Child Matters' agenda, reinforcing that if every child matters, every parent also has to matter.

Learning from the EPRA schools

This section draws on specific examples and illustrations from schools in the EPRA project. It aims to highlight the range of processes and strategies that EPRA schools have used to enhance and extend parental engagement. These examples fall into four broad categories and, it is argued, are most successful if underpinned by a shared whole school ethos and shared understanding that all parents matter and are valued and respected.

The four broad areas of activity reflected in the examples that follow are:

1. information and reporting
2. communication and dialogue
3. involvement
4. engagement.

This section concludes with a range of school case study examples that illustrate how a rigorous, whole school approach to parental engagement can emerge from small, focused activities aimed at raising achievement and maximizing student outcomes. The central point here is that parental engagement is not a 'bolt on' extra, but integral to teaching and learning.

Many barriers to parental engagement are surmountable if there is the *will, skill and persistence* to engage parents. The benefits of committing time and energy to engaging parents in learning are worthwhile and far-reaching. This is the most powerful lever we have if we are serious about raising achievement. The challenge is to use it. All the EPRA schools have added significant value to student learning and achievement through focusing their energies and time on effective engagement with parents.

1. Information and reporting

Many schools on the EPRA campaign found it useful to focus their energies on reviewing the way they presented information to parents. Traditional communication methods such as newsletters, handbooks and letters home can often be ineffective methods of communication. This is because many parents do not take the time to read them. Secondly, many parents find the information inaccessible or irrelevant to their child and, thirdly, in our high tech world, the predominant mode of communication is no longer paper-based. While school websites and eportals offer a potential solution, getting the content right is as important as with more traditional communication methods. Many schools in the EPRA project have developed new ways of working with parents and students by using podcasts, DVD clips and images with text to increase accessibility. The schools have also worked on getting the content right, so parents find time to read the information.

Enabling as many parents as possible to access information is an important first principle of parental engagement. If you are not communicating with parents effectively, how can they engage? Schools in the EPRA project looked at various ways of getting timely and important information to parents. Approaches included newsletters, student post, text messages, targeted post to parents, use of online media. All the schools agreed that increasing the different routes and forms of communication has ensured that they now reach more parents.

One of the best resources within the school is actually parents themselves. Often these can be overlooked and underutilized, but their potential to offer advice and guidance about effective communication with parents is enormous. One EPRA school employs a team of mealtime supervisors for an additional three hours a week to look at the language and content of various newsletters, letters home, contracts, parent resource packs and online materials. Their work includes translating content into the main community languages and ensuring that all parents can access the information. The school has found this to be a useful way of breaking down potential misunderstanding and overcoming resistance from parents.

Alder Grange School has produced a thorough 'one stop shop' guide for parents as the new handbook. This handbook contains everything parents need to know about the school, explores how parents can support learning, outlines the curriculum and national education initiatives, and gives directions for support, advice and guidance. The language is accessible and the content relevant. The handbook has been praised by Ofsted and has been positively received by parents.

The parent group working on the handbook have subsequently recommended additional ways that the schools could inform and communicate with parents, e.g. credit card sized handouts that provide term dates and key contact information, and leaflets about current issues and challenges.

Astley Community High School invited parents to a parental partnership meeting to discuss the content of the parental handbook. The school targeted parents and sent a personal invite to the meeting to try to increase engagement of all parents, but of fathers in particular. As the handbook focused primarily on helping parents to understand school processes and procedures, it was important that it was so well received by parents.

Great Sankey School have developed 'parent services', which is a school version of 'customer services' providing information, advice and support in one place. By using parent services, parents can access general information about the school and specific information about their child. 'Parent services' is both a paper and online resource provided for all parents that is regularly updated and refreshed.

Across the EPRA schools, a wide range of media are currently being used to inform parents about key points in a student's academic life, e.g. transition, revision exams. Parents are actively involved in reviewing materials to ensure they are written in accessible language and that they meet the needs of different families with different cultural backgrounds.

For many EPRA schools, e-portals and parent gateways have been invested in and developed. These initiatives have transformed schools' ability to provide parents with access to up-to-date information on their child's progress, attendance, punctuality, homework. A wide range of technologies enable the provision of routine information without onerous demands on staff time. In addition, these IT developments have allowed both parents and staff access to the same range of data. The jump many schools have made from simply *providing* information to enabling parents to *use information to enhance learning* has made a considerable difference to the way parents support learning in the home.

At Cramlington High School, a 'parent partnership' meeting

identified a group of 30 parents who agreed to trial the use of ICT to improve home-school communications. Parents were offered access to staff via direct email addresses and were given access to data on predicted grades and other information through an eportal. This form of communication is working well and both parents and staff like the direct communication it provides.

Alder Grange School introduced its online 'Parents' Gateway' to give parents secure access to their child's data. A series of training events were also provided to enable parents to access and understand the data provided. There is evidence of positive effects on behaviour, attendance and achievement as parents feel that they have timely and appropriate information to be able to help their child's learning in the home.

Bury Church of England High School has also launched an e-portal called the 'Parents' Gateway'. This gateway is a web-based secure system for parents to access information about their child, including information on attainment, attitude to learning, attendance, punctuality and behaviour. A series of events prepared parents to access and use this information to support their child's learning.

The Compton School has focused its efforts on helping parents get the most out of its eportal by offering ICT training and drop-in sessions. By working with parents, the school produced an accessible guide to the e-portal that focuses on academic attainment and achievement. In addition, out of hours access to computers is provided for parents with no home access to the internet.

Warden Park School aimed to improve attendance and punctuality by creating a more immediate means of reporting absence. This was facilitated by a restructuring of the pastoral system. Each year group has a 'Director of Progress and Learning' who works with a learning mentor as the first point of contact for parents. The parents of students who do not register in the morning are contacted immediately by the learning mentors. The impact of this approach has been significant and has resulted in improved attendance across all the year groups.

At Greenford High School, attendance has been improved by employing a dedicated attendance officer who leads and manages an automated system to inform parents if their child is not in school. The parent has a specific contact number so that any issues can be addressed rapidly. A sister system alerts parents to meetings and parents evenings dates. This approach has increased attendance rates and parental participation in meetings significantly.

A number of other schools are also exploring text messaging as a way of improving information flow to parents. Text messaging approaches tend to be used with a focus on attendance and punctuality. Lytham St Annes Technology College has introduced a text messaging service that sends messages to parents that range from congratulations for effort/good work, to reminders about important dates and highlighting potential issues/problems.

Westwood School wanted to develop its use of technology to improve achievement, attendance and punctuality. The 'Text-Magic' project has involved reporting by text to parents on a weekly basis. Parents report that they were highly appreciative of the regular and specific contact. Similarly, Oakmeeds Community College has used text messaging to keep in regular communication with parents of targeted disaffected students.

EPRA schools clearly identified the positive benefits of providing parents with accurate and relevant information. Homework has been a consistent focus of many different forms of communicating with parents. Homework has been reported as a frequent source of conflict between parents and their children, therefore many schools aimed to focus on this particular issue (Crowley 2006). Electronic and written communication has been used to provide information to parents about what homework is set, when it is due and what it aims to achieve. This clarification removes any misunderstanding as it provides a shared information base for parents and young people to talk about homework and learning.

Chelmer Valley High School has piloted the setting of homework and emailing it to parents. The email explained the objectives for the homework, how to complete it and set clear deadlines. Students or parents were encouraged to subsequently email back the work, or send it via the online learning platform Kaleidos, which allows interaction between teacher and student over the web. This particular development has had a positive impact on the amount of homework successfully completed, and has improved levels of parent/teacher interaction about homework matters.

The Headlands School improved communication about homework by introducing information sharing via booklets, meetings and web-based information. This approach has removed some of the tension around homework as students *and* parents know exactly what homework has been set, when the hand-in day is and what the objectives are for the home work. A similar approach has been adopted at Rising Brook College where school staff work with parents to provide parent friendly homework packs to help support learning in the home.

It is clear that when schools complement meaningful and relevant information about the child *with* access to a key member of staff, the impact on student learning is significantly enhanced. Many schools on the EPRA campaign have therefore appointed new colleagues with a specific brief to:

- build trusting and respectful relationships with parents
- use information and communication with parents to help them in helping their child learn
- engage with targeted parents, specific groups of parents or key community groups.

Deptford Green School has employed an academic mentor to work with the local Vietnamese community. Lack of English and low literacy levels were identified as significant barriers to many Vietnamese parents accessing learning opportunities. With support from the Ethnic Minority Achievement Service and other agencies, the school has been able to run an entry level course in English with computer skills. This was held on Saturday mornings with support from the Vietnamese-speaking Academic Mentor. Many of the attendees were parents of children at the school.

Central Foundation Girls School addressed specific needs of their community by appointing a Bengali-speaking 'outreach worker' as a key link for parents. She was able to encourage parents to attend classes and engage with the school through a parent's forum group.

Bowring Community Sports College introduced a 'parental partnership team' as the single point of contact for everything (other than routine absence reporting). This team also had responsibility for primary liaison with parents from Year 6, and for input to, and organizing, 'parent engagement days' to target challenging students and their parents.

Kelvin Hall School provided parents with a single point of contact, a direct telephone line to the Attendance Office and Student Support Coordinators. This provided quick response to calls, which parents welcome, and feedback showed parents felt it had made the school more accessible and parent friendly.

The Morton School introduced 'key workers' employed from the local community to improve communication and links with parents. Teachers have welcomed this initiative, as it has enabled them to focus on learning. The key workers are positive advocates of the school in the local community, and parents report feeling comfortable in approaching them. Teachers and key workers work together to target and identify which students and their parents to work closely with.

Feltham Community College produced a Parents' Handbook aimed at Year 7 parents. They also engineered a team of non-teaching staff called 'Parent Pals' to provide a single point of contact for certain students and their families. The Parent Pals inform parents of progress, successes and pass on times and dates of important events and deadlines. Parent Pals liaise with staff to solve any issues arising: not completing homework, attendance or punctuality concerns and not meeting academic targets.

Westfield Community School appointed a Parent Support Advisor to identify disengaged parents, and then work on breaking barriers through home visits and coffee drop-in sessions, to create a sense of mutual trust between home and school. The aim was to use the parents who were initially targeted to become the driving force behind drawing in other previously disengaged parents.

What does effective practice in informing and communicating with parents look like?

- Parents are provided with *accessible information* about their child's progress, which enables two way communication.
- Parents have *access* to a member of staff if the parent wants to review their child's progress and the factors that may be helping or hindering this progress.
- Attendance and punctuality are accurately and consistently. *recorded*, and parents know the system of sanctions and rewards
- There is *prompt and proactive contact* with parents to identify and action concerns.

The second strand of communicating effectively with parents is effective reporting. Online reporting to parents is now an *expectation* for all schools. This expectation has heightened schools' commitment to getting it right and providing information in an accessible, relevant form for parents. Once again, the key imperative is enabling parents to access and use information in dialogue with their children. This dialogue can be enhanced by building positive relationships between school and home.

Sale Grammar School has developed an iReporting system

allowing parents access to up to date information on their children. This has enabled regular parental, subject and school tracking to be shared between school and home along with discussions at academic review days about meaningful target-setting. Parental feedback suggests that they now feel more aware of expected standards and are better prepared to help their children.

Bushey Hall School wanted to engage more parents in the school community through an eportal and the school website. Parents were given access to data regarding attendance, lateness, commendations and sanctions, and both parents and the school report significant positive benefits for students from this improved information flow.

Cardinal Wiseman Catholic Technology College introduced an iReporting system as part of a wider process of developing communication with parents. As well as weekly and half-term newsletters, parents have access to detailed information about attendance, punctuality, performance and behaviour. Parental response to the innovation has been positive.

The Mirfield Free Grammar and Sixth Form College has developed a SIMS system that includes parental access to a new learning gateway. This gateway provides up-to-date information about attendance, punctuality, achievement and target grades. Parents have been provided with support and guidance from the school about accessing and using the data. The impact of the initiative on levels of parental engagement has been positive.

What does effective practice with reporting look like?

- *Explicit links* are made between what is reported and how this impacts on student learning.
- Parents have been engaged in the *development and communication of reporting* and are comfortable about what is being reported, how it is reported and how this can enhance learning.
- The accessibility and usefulness of reporting is *regularly reviewed* with parents, students and staff and feedback is acted upon.

2. Communication and involvement

Parental communication and involvement in the life of the school are important because both foster positive and respectful working relationships. They also serve to challenge long held negative perceptions and by involving parents in school activities there are opportunities for families to socialize as a group within the wider school community.

Schools have a key role to play in supporting community cohesion in an equitable and supportive way. Parental involvement activities can move parents and schools towards eliminating barriers to learning. As previous chapters have reinforced, however, moving from parental *involvement* to parental *engagement* is important if learning in the home is to be maximized.

Historically, schools have provided wide ranging opportunities for parental involvement from PTA-run school fetes to staff-led quiz nights. Parental involvement can be secured in a variety of ways. For example, a sample of approaches schools use include targeting parents and sending individual invitations by letter, phone call or text; using a range of media to advertize and market, from local paper adverts to posters in the local shops; offering incentives for attendance; using parents and students as recruiters and finally, advertizing on the website with a follow-up email. The more methods used to advertize and recruit, the more parents will attend.

At Meole Brace School, Barnardos has been running a series of courses for parents entitled 'Living with Teenagers'. The course offers families support in communicating effectively and confidently with young people. The course has provided a forum for increasing parental involvement and communication with the school. The courses have focused on topics such as adolescence, living together, managing anger and stress, and substance awareness. Follow-up questionnaires to participants have showed that parents felt better informed and more able to support their children as a result of the programme.

At Castle View School, the Pastoral manager has organized a family sports morning and a cycle training course, both intended to encourage families, especially fathers, to become involved in sports activities. Students and their families were also invited to attend six hours of first aid training run by St John's Ambulance. This course was highly successful, as parents and their children worked together to achieve their first aid certificate. The feedback showed that all participants had enjoyed the experience and felt very positive about gaining skills that could save lives.

At Haling Manor High School, many of the parents and students are second language learners. In response to the data contained in student questionnaires, the school arranged a wide range of social events for parents and students with food as a main focus. The events included 'Master Chef' parent and child cookery courses, quiz evenings and family food-and-fun nights. These events helped raise cultural awareness and were successful in increasing the number of parents coming into the school. The school wanted to utilize these evenings to emphasize key messages about learning in a fun and engaging way. The majority of parents expressed the view that the evenings were enjoyable and had reinforced the need for a closer relationship between parents and the school.

Pershore High School has run a number of workshops supporting parents of disaffected children. Parents were encouraged to meet in supportive and unthreatening environments, sometimes non-school-based, to participate in groups such as 'surviving teenagers', 'hooked on a book' and 'click onto ICT'. Local authority and school staff were available to refer to support agencies if necessary. Parents were actively recruited by adverts at school, in the local media, and individually by telephone, at student review meetings and parents evenings.

At Ramsay College, a 'surviving GCSE' evening for parents of KS4 students was well received and covered diverse topics, including study skills, post-16 opportunities, discouraging smoking and keeping teenagers fit, in addition to curriculum subjects.

Hamstead Hall School runs a programme of extended school activities from 8.00 a.m. until 5.30 p.m. every day and through the holidays. Students attend the 'Teacher Free Zone' and parents are encouraged to utilize parenting classes, health, legal and financial support facilities. The school is active in helping single parents return to work by offering skills training and using a recruitment agency at parents evenings and other gatherings.

What does effective practice with partnership opportunities look like?

- Supportive parent partnership activity is a feature of the school, and parents are actively *encouraged to join in*. This is evident through parent feedback.
- A range of forums supports this ethos with *targeted and volunteer parents* joining in through the Parents' Council, Parents' Working Group, Parent Governors, PTA, Friends, etc.
- Parents actively *recruit other parents* for this, and opportunities for joining in are embedded through the school plan.

Section 2 of the Self Evaluation Framework requires schools to provide evidence about their commitment to gathering, collating and acting upon parental feedback. This includes presenting evidence to show how parental engagement is improving overall provision. It is clear that schools can use positive parental feedback to share and celebrate, and they can use constructive feedback to target areas for further improvement.

Active and supportive parent forums, councils and working groups are a positive feature of a progressive and forward-moving school (Harris 2007; Epstein 2002). In chapter 5 we address some of schools' fears and challenges in managing and leading these groups to enable positive and effective outcomes. The examples that follow explore a range of ways schools have embraced working with parents to positively move the school forward. Schools report that using the Self Evaluation Framework as a scaffold ensures that parental feedback is acted upon, and that there are processes in place to feedback on this action to parents. Forums, councils and working groups are an effective route for this feedback to be channelled to parents informally. Further ideas for formal feedback are explored below.

As a new school, Bradley Stoke Community College worked with parents in developing reporting. Parental focus groups provided feedback and reactions to different systems, so that the final model was one welcomed by all. It conducted a training needs survey, and responded with relevant courses for parents ranging from web design to Indian head massage. The parental focus groups are now a feature of all development activity at the school.

Etone Community School audited their current activity with parents and surveyed parents to glean their views on how to improve engagement. A focus group of staff, governors and parents developed the feedback as a series of proposals designed to increase parental engagement with learning.

Glenthorne High School has made efforts to involve staff, students and the community in its planning of extended services and activities. It ran successful courses for parents of teenagers, hosted a performing arts careers evening and ran a 'Living and Learning Transition' project, which led to an active and popular Year 7 parent council. The school runs a wide range of adult and family learning activities, as requested and co-managed by the parent council.

Longcroft School recognized that parents don't always understand school processes, and that traditional ways of explaining school processes are not always accessible. The school works with parents to help remodel existing programmes and information.

The newly formed Oriel High School created a Parent Support Group (PSG) to represent parents and be closely involved in the planning and development of the school. The PSG have produced a high quality new parents' handbook and a regular 'Parents4Parents' newsletter; they run parents' drop-in clinics and have initiated a rolling programme of parents' information evenings, including 'dads' evenings', and a life-skills coach is supporting with workshops throughout the summer and autumn terms.

What does effective practice look like in working with parents?

- Parents are actively involved in reviewing all aspects of school, e.g. policies, uniform, discipline through Parent Council/Parent Working Group. Action is taken on information gleaned and fed back to parents.
- Action is taken in response to parental feedback.
- There is a systematic approach to ensure parental views are listened to and acted upon, and the school regularly feeds back to parents and seeks further feedback on action taken.
- Parental feedback demonstrates that these systems are embedded and effective.

We assert through the book that it is effective parental *engagement* that determines an impact on learning and outcomes. A number of schools see the first stage of this as involving parents in their child's learning. Involving and informing parents about their child's academic progress, their successes and achievements, issues affecting performance or attendance or punctuality leads to respectful, meaningful relationships between school and home.

Parents that are well informed of all aspects of their child's performance and well-being in school are then in a position to take this involvement to the next stage: *engagement with the child's learning*. These following examples emphasize the importance of communication and dialogue in encouraging partnership approaches and engaging them in supporting students through working with and alongside parents.

Sion Manning RC Girls School targeted a group of students that were demonstrating challenging behaviour. The school aimed to empower these students by working with their parents to maximize their academic potential. Weekly meetings with senior leaders, weekly student/parent workshops, student one-to-one interviews, and employing a professional Caribbean businesswoman to act as a role model, were strategies adopted by the school. Students and staff now report that the group are more focused, with the number of behaviour logs reduced by 79 per cent.

The parents of eight underachieving students were targeted by St John Bosco Arts College, and their parents were offered a parenting programme and support. The emotional needs of the students were addressed by a psychotherapist. As a result, parents felt more confident and gained increased skills and strategies to use with their children in difficult situations, and the students' behaviour and attitudes to learning improved.

In an effort to increase the engagement of parents of disaffected key stage 3 students, Romsey School offered 'Positive Parenting' classes to parents of Year 6 and 7 students. Parents were also invited to shadow their children for a morning when they entered as Year 7 students. A targeted group of Year 11 parents met with the mentoring team to maintain good communications over their children's last three terms in school. Parental access to school ICT and VLE systems was encouraged by staff-run sessions for parents. A number of family events, including a 'National Women's Day', an activity day and a 'build your own computer' initiative, encouraged some previously disengaged parents into school. All initiatives were managed and coordinated by a parental strategy manager on the SLT.

To fully support students at key points in their school career requires partnership working between home and school. Providing parents with quality information *and* access to staff in school enables parents to support their child at home. Transition from key stage 2 to 3 is identified as particularly stressful for parents as they see their children go from a small primary to the unknown world of secondary school (Crowley 2007). The support the secondary school can provide for parents is a longer term investment in this key relationship. Providing relevant and meaningful support *and* information at this stage set expectations about what a parent can anticipate from the school, what the secondary school expects from parents and how the partnership can be highly effective for the student.

Ashton Community Science College appointed a 'parental engagement officer' to liaise with the pastoral team and work with local feeder primaries at transition. The focus is to engage parents of students with low attendance and challenging behaviour. The students and their parents were invited to a three-day football school as an informal opportunity for parents to interact with the pastoral team, alleviate some of the concerns around transition and setting clear expectations for life at secondary school.

John of Gaunt School aimed to engage with all parents of Year 6 ahead of their start in Year 7. They used wide ranging strategies including newsletters, visits by staff, team teaching specialist subjects, co-led transition unit drop-in sessions, open days, home visits and access to the eportal.

Fakenham High School funded a member of staff to improve the website and to build links with local primary school websites. Parents were emailed with a question that required them to find information on the school website for the chance to win a cash prize. This increased numbers of parents visiting the site. Staff went 'on the road' to visit all feeder primary schools (wide locations) and invited children and their parents to visit them to learn more about the school.

What does effective practice look like in communicating with parents?

- Whole school policies are in place and are written in consultation with parents.
- Parents have access to information about their child's attitudes to learning and behaviour through a range of media and know how to use and understand the information.
- There are systems and processes in place for regular communication with parents to emphasize positives: recognizing and celebrating student success, and targeting groups and individual parents to highlight these successes.
- Events to celebrate success are planned through the school year and clearly communicated to parents through a range of media.
- The school holds wide ranging celebration events to engage different groups of parents, including some off site provision. These are well attended by parents.
- Parent and student review and feedback is built into a yearly plan and informs future events and activity.
- There are systems and processes in place to involve parents at an early stage with concerns on progress and behaviour. Strategies to support the student are negotiated, agreed and implemented with parents in the majority of cases.

Engaging parents to raise achievement   **43**

- Parenting sessions are provided for parents of students in different year groups addressing the age-specific issues that parents have raised through feedback.
- Targeted parents are invited to attend these sessions to further support their child.

3. Engagement with learning

In chapter 1 we outlined three different processes for engagement and learning:

- Parental engagement *for* learning
- Parental engagement *through* learning
- Parental engagement *about* learning.

This section explores how schools have attempted to move their involvement activity to focus on engagement *with learning*. Parental engagement *for* learning connects parents to curriculum content, classroom materials and resources. The main aim is to enable parents to understand what is being taught and the content of what is being learned. There is significant online potential here, schools with virtual learning environments have utilized these to provide materials for parents; these can be in written form and/or combine use of visuals, podcasting, DVDs, etc.

Parental engagement *through* learning describes the opportunities schools provide for parents as learners. It is the powerful combination in providing wide-ranging opportunities for parents to engage with learning that leads to greater potential impact on what happens in the home (Harris 2007), as these examples demonstrate.

Weaverham School designed a project involving making and racing model cars. The 'car club' met each week with targeted boys and a significant male. How the project supported the boys' learning was made explicit through each activity and session. Attendance to the club at 100 per cent proved its success; the boys showed an improvement in relationships in school, and feedback from dads, uncles and grandparents supported school feedback.

St Anne's High School invited parents to a number of evenings focusing on target-setting, supporting revision, explaining targets, progression and how achievement is related to good attendance. Activities were interactive and fun with key messages that this is to help and enable learning. Underachieving Year 11 students were targeted, and the school worked with parents to provide alternative provision for them.

Corpus Christi Catholic Sports College identified a group of underachieving Year 11 students. Parents were asked to a meeting with the personal mentor where they were asked to sign a diary each day to show discussions about learning and that agreed tasks had been completed. The mentor maintained frequent contact with parents to offer additional support. All students improved on their predicted grades.

The John Kyrle High School targeted a group of under-performing Year 11 students, and invited them and their parents to attend meetings designed to help parents understand how they could improve their child's GCSE results. The sessions were flexible, addressing parents' needs, and covered areas such as revision, learning styles, mind maps, time management, peer pressure and the home learning environment. The focus on learning gave parents practical skills and suggestions to use at home with their child.

The Gleed Girls' Technology College recruits from a diverse range of ethnic backgrounds, and needed to provide relevant and comprehensible information to a number of families with EAL. To encourage parents into college, the school provided a 'Portuguese' day, parenting classes, regular meetings with a translator present, academic review days and one-to-one support days. A comprehensive booklet giving wide-ranging information was provided for parents in an accessible format, and targets were set for each student. As a result, attendance has improved and KS3 students from EAL families are showing improvements in attainment. There has been positive feedback from parents who said they feel more comfortable approaching the school and more confident in helping their child with learning.

The Belle Vue School provides ICT skills sessions for mothers. The project is supported by Education Bradford who provide laptops that mothers are able to take home. The sessions are at a local venue and a crèche facility is provided. The project is designed to develop confidence in ICT skills in order to support their children's learning more effectively.

Stretford Grammar School changed the focus of their information and activity evenings to be far more about learning. Detailed and accessible information was given alongside practical ways in which parents can help their child with learning. Alongside this, the school targeted underachieving students and worked with their parents in finding the best ways to support their learning. The school reworked the newsletter and website, and increased email to increase the different ways the school communicated with parents. Personalized tours for prospective parents have enabled the school to take a personal approach from the first meeting with parents.

Campsmount Technology College introduced a revision support evening to enable parents to help their children learn. The event introduced parents to a range of strategies, so that they could select the ones they thought most likely to work with their own child.

The City Academy Bristol runs curriculum workshops in Maths, English and Science for parents of Year 7 and 8 students. Parents have fed back that they feel more confident in supporting their child's learning, and feel more confidence as learners themselves. The school has been successful in reaching out to Somali parents with well attended workshops on the English education system. These parents indicate that they have a better understanding of their role in supporting their child's learning.

Hornsea School & Language College formalized that learning is the focus of its revision workshops, transition events, and parent support programmes. Parents have noted that these events, the family learning events and courses run for parents as learners, have enabled them to discuss ways to learn at home and made them feel confident with this role.

At St John the Baptist School, parents of Year 11 students are invited to a compulsory evening to explore the best ways to work with their child through revision. Parents are provided with detailed resources from each department to use with their children at home. The school has moved towards making these compulsory to emphasize the important role parents have in supporting their child with revision.

Islington Arts & Media College appointed a member of staff to oversee a project to develop study support for parents, alongside an existing and successful study support program for students. This provision for parents covers issues such as transition, SATS and thinking skills. Sessions are repeated in the three main community languages, and the school has used a range of ways to advertize the sessions, target parents and ensure good attendance.

The Joseph Rowntree School worked with parents and students in setting targets for GCSE and providing detailed information about coursework content and deadlines. The school moved its mock exams for Year 11, so that the whole autumn term was devoted to coursework so school students and their parents could make this the focus. This has had a significant positive impact on the school's results at GCSE.

Salford City Academy completed a parental survey and, in response, offered computing and language courses with all facilities open to pre-school children (the toddler library). In addition, the information sent out to parents about preparing their children for exams was reviewed and improved. Parents needed support and encouragement to attend, and this was provided via individual telephone calls, offering lifts and providing a warm welcome.

The Berry Hill High School focused on targeting both parents and students of Year 9 and Year 11 by organizing a high profile progression evening and work fair. The project invited all local colleges, FE/HE establishments, training providers, employers and Connexions and was organized with the local Aim Higher. The event raised awareness of local training opportunities for parents to re-enter education or employment and enabled students with their parents to make positive choices for their futures. This project has raised learner aspirations and high-lighted wider opportunities for future careers.

Schools have pushed the boundaries with new technologies to look at providing shared learning opportunities with parents through different media. The use of podcasts and interactive discussion forums are illustrated in these examples.

Millthorpe School encouraged home learning through the development of podcasts where parents and students can discuss and enjoy reviewing learning together. This earned the school national recognition at last year's BECTA Exhibition. Wildern School has also created podcasts on their secure website to enable parents and students to access information on revision techniques from home and use it to work together and discuss ideas.

Chalfonts Community School provide online discussion forums for parents, with a curriculum and learning focus. This enables parents with internet access (the majority) to engage in revision and study evenings while sitting at home. Guest speakers and staff presentations are recorded on the web so if parents cannot access them at the given time, the presentations are there for them to look at 24/7. The same applies for the discussion forum content. Staff and parents have ongoing access to the discussions, so parents are free to ask questions and raise points outside times specified. Parents have welcomed this flexibility and have enjoyed being able to access curriculum content at the point they may be discussing this with their child.

What does effective practice with parental engagement look like?

- It is clear that the ethos of the school places learning at the core of all activity.
- Parents are supported in, and know and understand, the key role they play in their child's learning. This is evident through activity outcomes.
- There are explicit links to learning through all planned engagement activity and this is clearly communicated through a range of media to all parents and students.
- Parent and student learning styles are planned and catered for through all activities.
- Involving parents in adult learning is celebrated, and opportunities are provided in line with the school ethos to place learning at the core.
- There is evidence that adult learning opportunities have positive outcomes for parents.

In many cases, progress with the parental engagement agenda has been made by schools by refocusing traditional activities. These create small steps that rapidly expand into more wide-ranging strategies that ensure that parental engagement positively impacts across the school. The cases that follow in the next chapter illustrate how small changes can lead to significant and sustained changes with positive outcomes for student learning and engagement.

Questions
- How many parents have home access? What are you providing in addition?
- How logical is your reporting?
- What do you hope to achieve by the information you provide to parents?

Effective parental engagement in action $\boxed{4}$

Introduction

The overarching message about effective parental engagement is that it cannot be a 'bolt on', it has to be at the centre of all aspects of school life. The main message from schools in the EPRA project is, once the commitment to engaging parents in learning has been generated, momentum will quickly develop and extend into wide-ranging effective practice.

Schools in the EPRA project were soon asking the same questions: What do we hope to achieve from parental engagement in learning? What do we need to do to ensure we reach as many parents as possible? How can we make our efforts meaningful for all parents? How do we ensure that parental engagement impacts positively upon learning? For many EPRA schools, initial small-scale activities aimed at engaging parents soon extended to become a whole school commitment.

> It was the snowball effect and within a term, parental engagement was explicit through all our school plan priorities.
>
> (Clare Foster, Deputy Head, Alder Grange School)

EPRA schools approached parental engagement in very different ways, but the commitment from the head teacher, senior leadership team and/or a senior leader proved to be pivotal in moving this agenda forward. The case studies reinforce the centrality of supportive leadership in promoting effective parental engagement. In addition, three *key processes* were identified by schools as essential for developing effective parental engagement. These were as follows:

1. Articulating a clear vision and purpose for this work
2. Commitment to getting all staff on board

3. An audit of existing practice to set future development plans.

These three processes will now be outlined in more detail with illustrations and examples from EPRA case study schools.

1. Clear vision and purpose

A clear vision and purpose about parental engagement is essential for effective practice to occur. In schools where this has been achieved there is a shared view that:

- *every* parent genuinely matters
- *every* parent is reachable.

Hope Valley College is committed to achieving 100 per cent engagement of parents. This target was set for all parents evenings and, in particular, for the parents of the 30 per cent of Year 10 students predicted to not achieve five or more GCSEs. The drive to achieve 100 per cent parental engagement required a multi-faceted action plan. It necessitated personalized contact, rigorous monitoring and follow-up, offering alternative opportunities, taking school out to the community, being flexible with meeting parents and negotiating phone call times. Using a range of ways to communicate with and personalize engagement with parents has resulted in improved levels of parent participation.

Reaching all parents undoubtedly takes time and commitment. It requires sustaining the engagement of those parents already on board, and working with these to find better ways of engaging other parents. It also requires thorough planning and personalized approaches to work with specific parent groups or individual parents.

Warblington School has worked with student ambassadors to ensure that communication opportunities and information for parents are accessible and relevant. The student groups work with their own parents to explain education jargon and to ensure that all communication is presented clearly.

At Slough Grammar School, a parent committee was set up to facilitate communication between the school and parents. Twilight and Saturday morning briefing sessions were held to support parents in assisting their child to learn. These sessions included subject-specific inputs, welcome to GCSE sessions, option choices for GCSE and a guide to staying on in the sixth form. These briefing sessions for parents focused primarily on supporting students' learning and have been extended to include target setting.

Aston School has been working with its 'already engaged' parents to look at ways of engaging other parents. As advocates and recruiters, parents put forward ideas, and most recently they have addressed the issue of engaging hard to reach parents. Attention was placed on creating strategies to break down barriers to engagement, using parents to recruit other parents from the local community.

Riverside Business and Enterprise College have employed a number of strategies to encourage parents to engage with the school. These have included producing colourful newsletters, text messaging to remind parents of events, a Polish speaker to overcome language barriers, an evening open to all members of the community with prize draws, individual parent invitations to termly award assemblies that include refreshments, and a parent friendly room. The numbers attending parents evenings have significantly increased, and engaged parents are now recruiting other parents to participate and contribute.

As highlighted earlier, parents identified, for whatever reason, as 'hard to reach' often find the school 'hard to reach'. Consequently, schools need to break down the barriers to engagement and this involves using different ways of communicating and recognizing that each parental group is diverse and often culturally mixed.

Longcroft School paid students in Year 10 to deliver the 'new look' glossy newsletter to local residents. The professionally presented newsletter was supported by local businesses, and advertising space was provided in the newsletter in exchange for a small amount of sponsorship.

Boundstone Community College has created a system for parents to speak to tutors directly about students' progress. Tutors were given allocated parent contact time on their timetable. Each tutor was supplied with a mobile phone to make the calls. Tutors and parents have reported the positive benefits of regular contact and this has improved relationships and parental support for learning.

Clearly articulating the school's central purpose in working with parents to support learning is important. So too is the commonly held belief that every parent is reachable. By setting a target of reaching and engaging every parent, many schools have embarked on ambitious and imaginative approaches that have worked.

What does effective practice look like?

- Parents and the school share ownership and commitment to the achievement of every child.
- Parents are meaningfully engaged with school development.
- Parent feedback and input is a welcome feature of all activity.
- Parental engagement impacts positively on learning (and behaviour and attendance).
- Processes for targeting specific groups and individual parents are embedded through all engagement activity planning.
- A wide range of media are used for communication with parents.
- Home visiting and outreach activity complement each other and reinforce the range of other practices aimed at engaging parents.
- Engagement rates by parents are high and plans to engage disconnected parents remain a high priority.

2. Commitment to getting all staff on board

Getting all staff on board is an essential ingredient in moving any agenda forward. Although school staff may be broadly supportive of the need to work in partnership with parents, there can also be some fear of 'parent power', often construed as parents wanting to impose their views too strongly. Challenging some of these deep-seated fears, and seeing the wider potential for a partnership with all parents, is a process most schools have to consciously undertake. It is possible to alleviate the fears of some staff about working with parents, but this requires two-way communication as the following examples illustrate.

Sponne School identified a small cohort of students who were responsible for a high percentage of call-outs and fixed-term exclusions. To positively engage the parents of these children in school life, a team of staff agreed to work exclusively with this parental group. The two-way contact was positive and solution-focused. Parents were invited to work with staff at a parent forum and to explore the interventions needed to support their children. The forum devised a series of student- and parent-focused sessions. One popular session, 'Horrible hormones!', was launched by a celebrity to encourage more parents to attend. As a result of these sessions, many staff found they had more opportunities to reward students and to communicate this positively to their parents. The number of call-outs for the target group of students reduced by 50 per cent over three terms.

Case Study

One school wanted to revisit and rewrite the school's behaviour, rewards and sanctions policies. The senior team were keen to engage the parents and student councils in this review and rewrite, but although staff welcomed student involvement, they were reticent to work with parents. There had recently been complaints from local residents about poor behaviour to and from school. There were also complaints about litter and vandalism from parents along with concerns about how the school managed challenging behaviour.

Staff felt that any forum to discuss behaviour would focus on the negatives. The senior team worked closely with union representatives to co-plan the event to reassure staff it was a worthwhile activity. Time and energy were spent inviting those parents who had expressed dissatisfaction and ensuring there was good attendance. Parents were made to feel comfortable and were given a positive welcome.

Parents were divided into groups and given a clear set of questions to answer and a task to complete in a short time:

1. What does outstanding behaviour look like: a) in class; b) around school; c) in the local community?
2. What behaviour approaches do you like and why?
3. Devise an ethos statement: what do you want a behaviour policy to do in this school?

Groups then provided feedback to the forum and, over the break, the leading teacher collated the ethos statements into a paragraph.

The groups were asked to adapt the paragraph and add the positive examples they had discussed. Below this they were invited to say what defined outstanding behaviour. The forum agreed that this work would provide the basis for the school's behaviour policy. Parents were asked to volunteer to run future sessions. These parents recruited other parents to the follow-up session. ⇨

The buzz of enthusiasm generated in the second forum was highlighted on the website, and the feedback to staff was overwhelmingly positive. The positive outcomes from the forum persuaded staff that this had been a risk well worth taking and it had created momentum for working with parents to find solutions to other key challenges the school faced.

What does effective practice look like?

- A shared vision and purpose for parental engagement is consistently recognised and reinforced in school action and development plans.
- Trusting, collaborative relationships are a feature of interactions between staff and parents.
- There is mutual respect for differences.
- Staff support each other to effectively engage with parents.

3. Auditing existing practice, future development plans

The third key process identified by schools as crucial in developing a whole school parental engagement agenda, is the need to audit current parental engagement practice and to actively plan for future development. Articulating a clear and purposeful vision and getting all staff on board needs to be followed by a rigorous review of current practice and decisive action planning and delivery.

Many schools in the EPRA project used an audit tool devised by The Compton School. The following extract from the audit entitled 'Helping learning take place' allows a school to record current practice and activity, to identify the evidence and to highlight what is left to do.

The fully developed version of the audit (see appendix 1) provides schools with one way of evaluating progress. By completing the audit, many schools found they could recognize gaps in provision and could also identify areas for development. Other schools used this audit 'tool' with parents forums and student groups to plan ahead. Schools also adapted, developed and amended the tool to suit their specific needs and context. Some schools aligned this audit tool with the Self Evaluation Framework to ensure that they were working towards 'outstanding' in all categories.

Helping learning take place:
What we provide for parents to enable them to support the learning of their child

	Impact	Evidence	Still to do
Year or subject specific information evenings: Intervention support evening for parents of students receiving support in the Core subjects	Students make better progress Parents are more able to offer guidance to students and support learning	Feedback forms ask specific questions about impact this will have on conversations about learning at home Parental feedback positive Parental requests for additional support and work Students requesting staff make contact with home	Consider stages to make relevant data available to parents Make information available in target language. Have specific support evenings for students on SEN register. Specific support evenings for EAL consider role of subject leaders. Consider timing of sharing Fischer Family Trust data

Willenhall School used the results of an extensive parental survey and audit of current practice with parents to create a clear plan of how to improve the home/school learning partnership. A 'learning partnership events calendar' was developed and traditional parents evenings were restructured as 'Welcome and Celebration Events'. In addition, a programme of family learning activities has been developed and implemented.

What does effective practice look like?

- There is high level commitment from parents by the careful. targeting by staff of certain groups and individual parents.
- A review and feedback process underpins year plans and informs follow-up activity.
- There are systematic processes used across the school to demonstrate that parental engagement activity impacts on student outcomes.
- There are interactive, thoughtful and accessible communication systems between home and school to collect feedback on the impact on learning.

Ways to engage parents

- Show a commitment to this agenda through the allocation of school resources. The creative use of resourcing makes anything possible. For example, having non-teaching pastoral leaders is a significant financial saving and can provide parents with a single point of contact available through the day without a teaching commitment. This can provide a rapid response to phone calls and queries.
- Members of the local community employed in school are positive advocates of the school and offer a positive voice in the community.
- Work with students to advance parental engagement activity. Students can advertize and market school activity and can be resident translators, proof-readers, advisors and advocates.
- Work with student groups in school. Student researchers at Wildern School wrote to all parents sharing their findings and suggesting how parents could follow up positive learning experiences through discussions at home.

$\Rightarrow$

- Review the welcome parents receive when they come in to school. A welcoming and parent-friendly reception area sends a clear message.
- Use your reception area (and other areas accessible to parents and visitors) as a place to celebrate parental engagement with the school and learning. Displaying a parent/visitor box in reception reinforces that parent/visitor feedback and views are important. Providing a tick box questionnaire that can be filled out while parents wait in the reception area enables feedback to be given when there is time. The questions can be tailored to meet the needs of the school and can include feedback on uniform, behaviour, noise levels, etc., and can vary according to any areas the school is keen to focus on.
- Including a space for visitors to comment on the welcome they have received, as part of the signing in process, will help indicate whether areas need development. Again this reinforces to visitors that they are welcome and that their views and input are important.
- Work with students and parents to give careful thought to names for events and activities run by the school. 'I'm a parent, get me out of here ...', 'Horrible hormones' and 'Keeping up with the kids' are titles that have appealed to parents, and these activities had good uptake.
- Check the sports calendar to make sure events don't clash with important football matches! Use wide-ranging methods to advertize, market and recruit to these events to ensure the effort and time that has gone into the planning pays off.
- Use the local press to highlight achievements of the school and send key messages to the local community about how much the school values parental engagement. Run stories that show positive impact of engagement activities and use these to market and advertize key dates and times.
- Find ways to work with parent volunteers. Student groups are especially creative with ideas and suggestions for this. Whenever there is a focus day in school, explore ways of encouraging parents to support and positively participate.

Questions
- How are your core values and beliefs communicated to parents?
- How will you reach all your parents?
- What is your vision and purpose for parental engagement?

Engaging parents in student learning: What we know

5

Introduction

As the previous chapters have clearly outlined, what makes a difference to student achievement is engaging parents in students' learning in the home. In this chapter, we look more closely at parental engagement in student learning by drawing upon the findings of the EPRA project. The chapter will examine what parental engagement actually means in practice and what prevents parents from engaging in learning. Finally, we'll offer some suggestions about what more schools can do to encourage and support parental engagement.

As highlighted in chapters 3 and 4, the EPRA[3] programme involved schools in innovative practice and developmental work aimed at engaging parents in student learning. During the life of the project study, the DfES (now DCSF) commissioned an independent evaluation of EPRA. This twelve-month multi-method study aimed to capture the impact of the project and to identify whether and how schools were engaging parents.

A research team collected data from students, parents and

---

[3] Note:
The EPRA research process involved 30 schools overall. In reporting the findings, schools were designated by a simple letter code, and respondents were listed simply by group (parents, staff, student) and, if appropriate, by role within those groups (head teacher, deputy, etc.). This was done to provide anonymity for the respondents, so that answers could not be traced to particular individuals. A fuller explanation of the research process and methodology can be found in the full report, Harris, A. & Goodall, J. (2007), *Engaging Parents in Raising Achievement: Do Parents Know They Matter?*, Department for Children, Schools and Families.

school staff in over 50 EPRA schools. The evaluation placed particular emphasis on the perspectives of parents and students. In this chapter we draw directly upon their views and evidence.

As noted earlier, research that has focused explicitly on the relationship between parental engagement and student learning (Harris and Goodall 2008) highlights that 'getting parents across the school threshold' can often be difficult. Activities focused on getting parents into the school tend to be premised on parents being reactive to the school's needs, rather than proactively seeking to be engaged in learning.

Findings from the EPRA project showed that parents were often expected to be responsive to schools, rather than being, or becoming, active participants and partners in learning. Schools frequently spoke of a triangle of *student, parent and school* – all involved in learning. Yet parents were often seen to be in reactive roles in relation to their children's learning, with schools directing the process of interaction. Involvement with the school and engagement with student learning are different but they are not independent processes. Both build on each other, but engagement with learning *in the home* should be the ultimate aim of all school and parental collaboration if there is to be a positive impact on student achievement.

Involvement v engagement

Parental engagement is an iterative process. It involves parents interacting with the school, parents interacting with their children, the school interacting with both parents and students, and finally with parents being engaged in the student's process of learning. None of these interactions stand alone; they affect each another. There is no one thing schools can do to ensure that parents engage since the process of communication between parents, students and schools is continual. If we were to plot this process, it might look something like this:

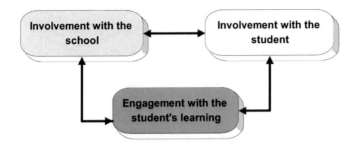

Through this ongoing process, parents will interact directly with the school by receiving reports, attending meetings, etc. Other times parents will interact with the student through, for example, discussions about things not directly related to school work, but still of importance to the student (see below), and at other times parents will engage directly with the student's learning by helping with homework or taking part in family learning events.

Involvement with the school through involvement in some school-led activity or as part of the PTA may be a necessary first step for many parents. It allows them to understand more about the school and the ways in which they can support their child's learning. Involvement may also mean the school giving parents information that will assist them support learning in the home, such as the content of course work, what is expected of students in terms of learning outcomes, or clear and timely reports on student progress; in short, whatever type of information will support learning in the home.

Schools may also help parents by providing them with opportunities to acquire particular skills, whether those are in relation to the content of what students are learning, such as classes for parents on maths or English, or joint learning activities for parents and children, or in relation to parenting itself through parenting classes, parental support groups, access to other agencies and means of support.

While these forms of parental involvement are important, it is engagement with learning that is the ultimate goal. However, getting there can involve different routes. It is important that schools 'get parents across the threshold', but the way they do so will inevitably vary.

The EPRA project found that some schools were clearly focused on parental engagement in learning. A number of schools had begun programmes of support for parents that were held in the community, rather than school venues. However, in the majority of cases, many events still tend to be held on school grounds and this reinforces the expectation that parents need to be responsive to the school.

When the EPRA research began, it quickly became apparent that the term 'parental engagement' was not something everyone could agree on; there were different definitions and different ways of seeing its purpose. It is clear that parents and schools may be using the same term but meaning something entirely different.

Differing views of parental engagement

In the EPRA project, parents and students tended to view engagement as broadly offering *support to students,* while school staff generally thought it was more about *supporting the school* in their work with students. This difference of opinion is often reflected in a dissonance between what parents and students want and what schools offer them. The different views of parental engagement can be illustrated as follows:

For school staff, the main purpose of parental engagement was the support that parents could offer *the school*, particularly in terms of improving behaviour. School staff hoped that parents would be involved in their children's learning by 'singing from the same hymn sheet' as far as behaviour was concerned. Staff expressed the desire for parents to support the school over issues such as attendance, uniform policies and homework, as well as behaviour in school. They were keen for parents to reinforce key messages they were giving about what constitutes acceptable behaviour.

Parents mentioned homework as one of the main ways in which they engaged with their children's learning. Parents reported that helping with homework was one of the ways they felt most able to support their child. Through being engaged in homework and course work, parents felt kept up to date with what their children were learning in school. Parents also felt that they could make a positive contribution to their child's progress and learning through helping with homework.

Students in the EPRA project talked about the moral support that their parents offered them as well as encouragement for their learning. While parents, students and the school clearly saw parental engagement as being about different things, the shared goal was clearly *improving learning*. In the next section, we'll examine why parents, students and staff felt that parental engagement was so important for learning.

Value of parental engagement

Parents, staff and students in the EPRA project responded to questions about parental engagement in two ways. The first focused on the practical issues of engagement, i.e. *what is it that parents actually do when engaging with their children's learning?* These issues included the practicalities of helping with homework or project work, or talking to children about how their day has been.

The second response concerned the *value* those actions have according to different groups of respondents – and whether they showed by their actions that education was valuable to them. It was clear that parents were much more likely to be engaged in their children's learning if they felt that education was important. The more parents *valued* education, the more they thought it was important, the more likely they were to engage with their children's learning and to be involved in the practical issues that surrounded it.

While the practical issues are clearly important, the EPRA study found that students highly valued the moral support parents gave and that they felt that this support directly influenced their subsequent academic achievement:

If they weren't interested, then you wouldn't be.

(Student, school D)

If they didn't want you to do well, then you wouldn't want to do well because it wouldn't make much difference.

(Student, school CC)

If they didn't want to come to parents evening, you wouldn't like have anyone pushing you.

(Student, school CC)

Some people's parents don't really get involved in their education and they aren't going to do as well – they aren't going to get a really good job because it all starts from here.

(Student, school Y)

I think it's your parents' recognition – I've lost my certificates now but I still know that my parents were proud.

(Student, school D)

Because if no one's involved, there's no point in doing it.

(Student, school N)

If they are involved then you're going to do well because you've got family behind you backing you up. If they're not involved you aren't going to do as well.

(Student, school Y)

Students told the research team, 'You can't do it alone'. The vast majority of students felt that the value of parental engagement was about moral support and acting as a role model, i.e. if parents value education, then the students were more likely to do the same. Students also reported that those of their peers who lacked parental support were considered less likely to do well academically. They were seen to be more likely to 'go off the rails', 'get in trouble' or to have to find moral support from their friends.

Most students in the EPRA study were not particularly interested in their parents' help with homework. In fact, older students were clear that their parents were unable to help in this way (a view echoed by parents, who often felt helpless or disempowered as a result). What mattered to students was not that parents were able to help with working through a maths problem, but that parents gave a clear message that education was important overall and showed an interest in education.

Students tended to take their cue about whether or not education was important from their parents, rather than from their teachers or their peers. Even when students did not want their parents to come into the school, insisted that parents drop them off well away from the school gates, and were reluctant to share much about school life at home, the fact that their parents actively took an interest in education was important to them.

One student in the research project who had received an award for effort pointed out that, although the certificates were important, it was more important to know that 'my parents were proud of me'. Other students were also clear about the connection between their interest in education and the interest of their parents. As one student highlighted, 'I want to do well for my mum, I'm doing it for her, really – otherwise there's no real point, is there?'

Parents in the EPRA study felt that their role was fundamentally concerned with providing moral support for their children's learning:

> It's not something a child can do alone – some of them do but it's much harder. I'm not really talking about academically – I'm talking about social and emotionally.
>
> (Parent, school T)

> I honestly think that a lot of parents do not spend enough time with their children. A lot of parents are spending less and less time with their children. They don't have time for their children. The parent might not realize how the child takes it. I think it breaks a bond. When the child gets older they will say, 'when I needed that help you didn't listen.' I think it's very important to keep emphasizing how important that is. Work is always going to be there. You bring them into this world and you should be a part of them until they are old enough to know what's right and what's wrong.
>
> (Parent, school T)

> It's part of growing up as well – if you hear other children say that their parents don't care – you know that your children can say, 'well, my mum and dad are there, my mum and dad help me.' It's very hard to explain but if you've got children who are brought up in a lovely family atmosphere, they know they're loved, they know their parents want them to do well at school, in my mind that child will do better than a child that doesn't get that attention..
>
> (Parent, school Q)

Both parents and students highlighted *moral support for learning* as the central purpose of parental engagement. This emphasis on the importance of education shows that parents and students shared a broad understanding that parental engagement was more than simply being involved with the school. They understood that it included a variety of things, from simply taking an interest in how a student's day has gone, through to help with homework, discussions about the student's future and educational options, to provision of study materials and other help with study. Effective parental engagement includes engagement with *the school*, engagement with *school work* and engagement with *learning*.

Parental support for learning was still deemed to be most important by school staff:

> There's no more powerful thing in education than a close working relationship between parent and child.
>
> (Head Teacher, school D)

> What I want to get across is that we're not just talking about physical involvement, it's hearts and minds that we're trying to get involved, that is what we're trying to do.
>
> (Head Teacher, school X)

Students made a clear link between their own achievement and their parents' support. As one student summed it up, 'If they're not bothered, why should I be?'

> Your parents are your main influence, really – if they don't care about it, you don't take as much of an interest in it.
>
> (Student, school V)

> If your parents aren't involved and don't really care, then you don't realize how important it is and then you just don't turn up to lessons and go downhill and that's it, and you sort of slide.
>
> (Student, school D)

> If the parents aren't bothered, then the child won't, which I don't think is good.
>
> (Student, school C)

> But some people, even if they do get like praise letters or bad letters, they [parents] don't really care and I think that's when you start going downhill a bit. If parents don't really care if you get good grades, then you start to lose interest.
>
> (Student, school D)

> If parents aren't bothered about a child's education, then I don't think the child would be bothered either.
>
> (Student, school Y)

These comments highlight the powerful relationship between parents' support for learning and the value students place on their own learning. Even when older students reiterated their need for space, and that parents could be 'clingy' or 'smothering', or apply too much pressure to perform well academically, there was no question but that they valued and actively wanted their parents to be interested in their learning.

Parents echoed the importance of the value they placed on education:

> If we had an attitude that it doesn't matter – why should they bother?
>
> (Parent, school D)

> You talk to kids about what they want for the future and how education is a step for that future, and it's, 'No you don't need an education – my mum says, my dad says, my brother never went to school and he's got a good job and it's only school and it doesn't matter if you don't get an education.'
>
> (Head of Year, school D)

Students reported that they wanted to please their parents, to gain their approval. They also made it clear that parental disapproval was a powerful force in managing student behaviour at school. Students who did not face parental sanctions were considered by students and staff alike to be far more likely to misbehave in school.

Behaviour and parental engagement

The EPRA study found that parental engagement had a direct and beneficial effect on student behaviour. When parents took no interest in student learning, or if there was no home-based consequence to bad behaviour at school, bad behaviour would continue. Communication between home and school on the subject of behaviour was found to influence the way students subsequently behaved in school and their responses to learning:

> Yes – we know we're not going to get away with it – other people might think they can get away with it.
>
> (Student, school C)

> If your parents had nothing to do with school, you could skip your lessons and nobody will be bothered. But if your parents are bothered,

then if you do something you think it won't be very good cause I'll get punished or I'll get my spending money taken off me.

(Student, school D)

Students tended to directly relate the level of interest their parents showed in their education to their behaviour in school:

You can tell the difference between someone whose parents are involved and when they're not. When they are involved you can see that like you work a bit harder, because you've got someone to realize that you are working harder. If my parents weren't involved, I'm not saying I'd go off the rails but I wouldn't be as bothered because there'd be no one to realize I was working hard, and you get that feeling that you've done well and they've seen it. The kids that come to school and don't wear uniform and don't follow rules – it's the parents in a way – if they just let you wear what you want and they don't check up on your homework, that's when you slide.

(Student, school D)

Parental engagement acts as a dual force, promoting *positive achievement* and reinforcing *good behaviour*; when parents show an interest in their children's learning, students are motivated to learn and to behave in ways that are more conductive to learning. Students told the project team that their behaviour in school was heavily influenced by their parents' reactions at home:

Parents should encourage their kids if they've done something well because then automatically the kid will want to do better to make their parents proud.

(Student, school V)

Students also linked parental interest in learning to parental care. When parents showed an interest in them and in what they were doing at school, students felt parents cared:

Yes – because they show that they actually care about you. If she didn't tell me that, I'd misbehave, I'd be out of the house.

(Student, school N)

Students also felt that it was important to reassure their parents, to let their parents know that they were doing well in school:

I think it's 'cause you're here for so long that they're doing something different at home and you're here and you want them to know that you've not gone off the rails and that you're still alright.

(Student, school D)

Parents – and most importantly students – were clear that it was the parents' views of *acceptable behaviour* that most often guided their behaviour in school. The importance of parental input was reiterated by a number of students, but perhaps best summed up by one student who declared, 'It's great when my teacher's pleased with me but your dad's your dad!'

Homework is perhaps the most obvious way parents can be involved in their children's learning and demonstrate the interest that is so important:

> If they're not doing homework, their academic performance is going to be lower and parental support is key in getting homework done.
>
> (Teacher, school Y)

Parents were engaged not only in the content of homework, but how and when it was assigned, how it related to learning overall, and whether children were doing the work and handing it in on time.

> Yes – it must, because if they know that their parents know what it is that they should be doing then they're more likely to do it and do it properly, whereas I think a lot of the time it's because the parents don't really know what they're doing because the kids aren't very talkative about what they're doing. But with this the parents have actually been here and have seen it and know what they should be expecting from their child and if they're not seeing that I would hope that they would take the necessary action which should ensure that they work a little bit harder.
>
> (Teacher, school EE)

Younger students placed more value on their parents' help with homework than older students. As students progressed through school, they frequently said that their parents 'couldn't' help or 'didn't understand what we're taught now'. This was echoed by parents, who discussed difficulties in dealing with the specific content of homework or coursework, but suggested their contribution could be a wider one: providing materials, trips out, checking on progress or due dates, or just showing interest in what their children were doing:

> It's difficult sometimes to sit down with a 14 year old – spend three quarters of an hour doing what? If you're working on an essay, you're talking about other things. And they're having you there, they're pleasing you, you're pleasing them and I think that's really important especially with so many.
>
> (Parent, school Q)

Helping with homework – either in terms of monitoring it or actively helping with it – came far down the list of overall activities valued by students. Students placed much more value on the interest that their parents showed in their learning overall and their providing moral support for learning.

For staff, the connection between the homework and learning was clear:

> If they're not doing homework, their academic performance is going to be lower and parental support is key in getting homework done.
> There's a definite knock-on effect on their overall attainment, yes. And their confidence in class as well – if they're not doing their homework and everyone else is contributing. There is a real boost, if they feel that they can do their homework, there's a huge boost in confidence.
>
> (Teacher, school Y)

Here again, there is a distinct difference between what students and parents emphasized and what school staff saw as most important. Parents and students reported that the main value of parental help with homework was that it showed that parents were *interested* in what their children were doing: it is primarily a way of being engaged in learning. School staff, however, saw the main value of parents supporting homework as making a direct difference to the *quality of that work*:

> Getting over that whole philosophy of what did you do at school – that goes nowhere, but asking what did you learn at school that's quite a deep question. How could you learn better at school today? What stopped you learning at school today?
>
> (Deputy Head, school X)

There are a number of messages that schools might consider from the research.

First that the agency, the power, the motivating force behind parental engagement resides with parents themselves. That does not mean that schools have no part to play in fostering or supporting parental engagement, or even in letting parents know how important their engagement in the learning of their children can be. It does mean, however, that schools need to recognize that parental engagement is not about *the school* but about strengthening the triangle of relationships between *school, student and parents*. It is clear that schools can support and foster that engagement, and where they do there are positive effects on achievement.

Secondly, involving parents with the school is not an end in itself, it is a means to securing engagement with learning. An integral part of that process is ensuring that parents have all the information they need, and in a form they can use, to support their children's learning. Information from schools to parents needs to be presented in a way that parents can understand and use. In the next section, we look at the idea of 'intelligent reporting', which is a powerful way schools can support parents' engagement with learning.

Effective reporting and communication with parents

Many schools have been working on new ways to report to parents, ranging from the high-tech solutions involving web access to school data and text messaging to low-tech solutions such as sending home postcards or making phone calls to report good work or outstanding progress. Some schools have seen remarkable results from new technological approaches to reporting:

> It has improved the attendance – it's gone up in 12 months nearly three per cent. We have the truancy call system ... [it] lets them [parents] know immediately.
>
> (Deputy Head Teacher, school H)

However, 'intelligent' reporting means not only accurate but also *useful* information; reporting that is *fit for purpose*, reporting that parents can *understand* (i.e. not laden with educational jargon, and terms are explained) and *use* to support their children's learning. There are (at least) two issues here:

1. What do schools need parents to know so that they can best support their children's learning?
2. What do parents need to know so that they can best support their children's learning?

> We're not asking teachers to do more to share the information you do hold – they have to record this stuff anyway – so if there was a website or something where we could see it – not a twenty page document.
>
> (Deputy Head Teacher, school Q)

Reporting to parents – no matter how 'intelligent', how accurate, how up-to-the-minute – is not the same as engaging them. Reporting is a one way process, as a student pointed out:

> Reporting is informing parents, not engaging them.
>
> > (Student, school C)

The parents we spoke with often talked about 'information overload' and difficulties in dealing with the language in reports from schools, i.e. 'teacher speak'. Parents reported receiving too much information and too little explanation about what to do with it.

> In terms of reporting, my husband doesn't understand it. He cannot understand it one bit. The reporting system is very complicated and it does need simplifying.
>
> > (Parent, school O)

Some schools were well aware of the problem:

> We can't talk about parents without talking about the data we're feeding parents. It's all very well telling them about the things going on outside of school, but if we're talking about getting parents involved with the education of their kids then what we've got to do is we've got to supply information to the parents that they can understand and help them interpret what we're saying about their kids.
>
> > (Deputy Head Teacher, school H)

While information is important, it is also clear that 'more is not always better'. What parents said they needed was simple, targeted information that told them clearly how their children were doing and what they as parents could do to support them.

The following diagram shows two forms of communication with parents – the first, being closed, needing little response from parents; the second being more open ended and allowing dialogue between parents and staff.

Closed communication is not necessarily a bad thing; there are things that all schools need to tell parents, rather than discuss with them. For example, exam timetables and the dates for school closures are not negotiable and therefore purely information that needs to be shared. In these instances, all the school needs to know is that the parents have received and understood the information given.

A two-way dialogue, however, suggests that parents need to respond to what is being said, either in writing or in person. This implies that some action will be taken depending on their response.

While most schools engage in both types of communication with parents, often the difference between them is not made clear. Inevitably, there are some things that are not open to

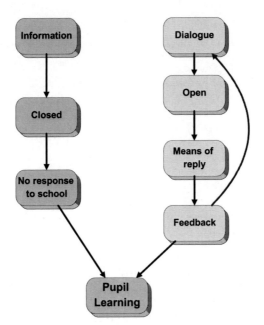

negotiation or discussion with parents. Parents just need to know what these are.

Intelligent reporting is one way of providing real time information on a child's progress, learning or attendance. It is direct information sharing but allows the parent to a) be informed in a timely way, and b) to offer appropriate support.

In terms of dialogue with the school and feedback, it is important to note that many parents lack confidence in their ability to engage with the work their children are doing. They may lack the social skills to operate within a school setting (or feel that they do). Schools highlighted examples of meetings where parents were clearly uncomfortable in a formal setting.

Also in terms of attending meetings, many parents may lack transport to reach the school, or the funds to do so; they may not be able to arrange childcare for younger siblings to allow them to come to the school site. This is particularly the case for rural schools that may have to plan evening events to fit in with local bus and train timetables. While technology may provide an answer to some of these problems, with the use of email and online reporting, this form of parental contact is not appropriate in all cases. There are times schools need to communicate face to face with parents. These might involve holding meetings in places other than school buildings or at other times of the day.

The school itself can also prove to be intimidating to some parents. The layout, even the presence of so many young people, can cause anxiety:

> I find it difficult to come into a high school ... It can be quite intimidating, you come to the office and that's quite intimidating – and you look at the kids as well, I'm not being funny, they're big, they're quite frightening – so I find it quite intimidating coming to a high school.
>
> (Parent, school D)

> It's just so big and vast. The school's huge... They go into the primary school but when they come here it's just too big – the crowd, the size, they feel intimidated not just by authority – the teachers – but the teenagers as well.
>
> (Teacher, school C)

Parents often feel cheated of the 'school gate' experience they had enjoyed at primary school.

> I think once they [the students] get past primary school where you leave them at the door, you lose them [parents] – you see them at parents evenings but that's about it.
>
> (Parent, school EE)

Parents' comments about the difference between primary and secondary school illustrated that it was not only the size of secondary schools that they found intimidating, but also their complexity. Many parents felt that they needed a 'road map' to negotiate their way around schools.

This barrier is one that schools will inevitably find difficult to overcome: a school that caters for a thousand students will always be a large, busy, imposing place. But there are ways to help parents navigate the complexity. These might include having a 'one stop shop' or a main contact for each parent so they know whom to go to, even if this person simply offers advice about the best person to talk to. Another way is a 'road map' of whom to contact about various issues. The more schools can help parents to make the right connections, the more likely they are to communicate with the school.

Many parents felt that there was a divide between parents and school staff. Some parents felt that it was a 'them and us' situation with parents and students on one side and staff on the other. Some parents perceived their role as that of protecting their children from the institution of the school. Possibly, this issue is related to parents' experiences of education or their expectation about how they will be treated in schools. Some parents explained that they had not been valued during their own education, so they had no pattern to follow in relation to the learning of their own children. Also, while students reported that they valued their parents' engagement with their learning, they also reported that there is a time and a place for such engagement – and for older students, at least, there was a strong feeling the school was not that place.

> It's a bit embarrasing. You want them somewhat involved but you don't want them coming into school when everyone's around. You want them to know what you're talking about.
>
> (Student, school P)

Other students made a distinction between being involved enough and overly involved:

> It's not too good when your parents get too involved and they get all clingy over what you're doing and every day when you get home they want to know what you're doing, what your homework is.
>
> (Student, school D)

Students reported an uneasy alliance between parental engagement in learning and parental presence in school:

> You want them to realize and take notice but you don't want them on your shoulder.
>
> (Student, school P)

Students often discussed a paradox between wanting parents to know about a school day, to experience a modern lesson and understand the atmosphere of the school, and being very opposed to having their parents present in school.

Students reported a need for space at school, i.e. away from their parents. Students expressed this in different ways, such as having a different personality at school than at home, being with peers and not wanting parents to encroach on their personal space. This need, however, was almost always juxtaposed with the continued need for (appropriate) parental support:

> You come up to comprehensive and the whole point of it is independence and you're totally thrown into a massive building and you don't know where you are, and [you get] tons of homework. You need your independence at this age but you also need your parents' guidance.
>
> (Student, school D)

This is a tension that most schools face and easy answers are in short supply. But it is clear that if schools can manage parents' presence in school, there are significant gains and benefits to learners.

Summary

Overall, there are some clear messages for schools that emerge from the EPRA research. The research shows very clearly that the ultimate goal of communicating with parents and involving them in activities in the school to secure their engagement is *learning in the home*. Getting parents into school may be a necessary part of securing engagement, but it is only a first step in the process.

It is clear that parents face many different barriers to engagement. As we have seen in the school examples in previous chapters, many schools are finding ways to overcome these barriers. Where this is achieved, it can make a considerable difference to student learning and achievement.

Questions
- What barriers to engaging with the school do parents in your school face?
- What barriers to being engaged in their children's learning do they face?
- Which barriers do you wish to address, and why?
- What activities does your school use to involve parents with the school?
- What means does your school use to communicate with parents?
- How effective are these communications in terms of their stated aims? Do any of them seek to support parents in engaging with the learning of their children?
- How 'parent friendly' is your school's reporting? What does it aim to do, and how well does it accomplish this aim?
- Do your parental engagement activities aim to engage parents with the school or with the learning of the children?

Where next?

Parental engagement seems to be the worst problem and the best solution. It is the worst problem because it can be difficult to secure, and it is the best solution in terms of raising student performance. While it is clear that parents play a vital role in securing better student outcomes, some parents still remain reluctant or unable to work with schools. As the EPRA research has highlighted, the aspiration of raising achievement can only be fulfilled if parents are *engaged in learning in the home*. It is also clear that differential strategies are needed to secure the engagement of a diverse range of parents.

There is evidence that parental engagement increases with social status, parents' income and level of education. So certain parents are more likely to engage in learning while others face certain barriers, influenced by context and culture, which can wrongly be interpreted as resistance or intransigence. Parental engagement is going to be possible with certain groups only if major efforts are made to understand the local community and if the relationship is perceived to be genuinely two-way (Harris et al, 2007).

As children get older, parental engagement from all social groups reduces. There are many reasons for this. First, parents feel that the child needs more independence as he or she gets older. Secondly, engaging with a large secondary school is not as easy as with a small primary school. Thirdly, young people can actively oppose engagement and can often feel embarrassed by their parents being in school.

While there are many good reasons for having parents in schools, it remains the case that their presence in school alone has little impact on learning. It might be good for social relations and to foster better links with the community. It might contribute to greater openness and accountability. However, to impact on achievement, parents need to engage with learning in the home rather than the school.

Parents are the most important influence on learning. Long after the early years gives way to formal education, parents continue to play a key role in student success and achievement. The lives parents lead today means that it is more challenging to secure their engagement in learning, but it still remains a factor that can make a significant difference to a child's educational attainment and subsequent life chances. Parents need to understand that they are an integral part of the learning process. They need to know they matter.

Parents who are already engaged in the learning of their children need as much support as those who are less engaged. The staff who work most closely with parents need not be teachers, and schools have to be prepared to be flexible in dealing with parents in terms of times of meetings (taking into account shift work, childcare issues) and, if possible, in terms of location. Most of all, schools must provide levels of guidance and support that enable engagement in learning to take place.

Without doubt, parental engagement in children's learning makes a difference and remains one of the most powerful school improvement levers that we have. But effective parental engagement will not happen without concerted effort, time and commitment from both parents and schools. It will not happen unless parents know the difference they make and unless schools actively reinforce their active engagement in learning.

Parents play a vital role in the development and education of their children and in the success of schools. Parental engagement in learning is a powerful vehicle for bringing teachers and parents together. It can help the school realize its potential and improve its outcomes.

For schools currently working towards greater parental engagement in learning, there are some important challenges and considerations:

- Parental engagement must be a priority – it cannot be a bolt-on extra. It must be embedded in teaching and learning policies, and school improvement policies, so that parents are seen as an integral part of the student learning process.
- Schools have to be clear about the aims of all communication with parents. Is communication in a given case meant to be open or closed? What response, if any, is required from parents, and how will that impact on the school and the learning of the child?

- Supporting the engagement of parents who are already involved in the learning of their children is as important as reaching those parents who are less engaged.
- Investment in training for staff who work most closely with parents is important; these staff members need not be teachers.
- Flexibility is required in face to face communication with parents, in terms of times of meetings (shift work, childcare issues) and, if possible, in terms of locations.
- New technologies can be helpful, but are only part of the solution. They are not an end in themselves.

All parents, regardless of income, education or cultural background, should be involved in their children's learning and want their children to do well. Schools are supporting this engagement through a wide range of innovative approaches that are making a difference to learning.

Supporting parental engagement in learning requires the design of approaches and programs to help families support their children's learning. This is not easy work but when effectively implemented can have a major impact on learning outcomes. Ultimately, effective parental engagement is premised upon building trust and mutually respectful relationships between the school and the home.

Coda

Schools are more effective where there is a stronger connection with parents as part of the learning community. The lives parents lead today means that it is more challenging to secure their engagement in learning. Yet this engagement can make a significant difference to a child's educational attainment and life chances.

Consequently, parental engagement needs to be at the core rather than the periphery of schooling. Parental engagement in children's learning makes a very big difference to learning. It needs to be centre stage. It is the most powerful school improvement lever we have. So let's use it. Parental engagement will not occur in a school without concerted effort, time and commitment on the part of both parents and schools. The real challenge, on both sides, is to make it happen.

Bibliography

Ball, M. (1998), *School Inclusion: The School, the Family and the Community*. York: Joseph Rowntree Foundation.

Birenbaum-Carmeli, D. (1999), 'Parents who get what they want: On the empowerment of the powerful', *Sociological Review*, 47, 1, 1–62.

Bogenschneider, K. (1999), 'Parental engagement in adolescent schooling: A proximal process with transcontextual validity', *Journal of Marriage and the Family*, 59, 3, 718–33.

Catsambis, S. (2001), 'Expanding knowledge of parental engagement in children's secondary education: Connections with high school seniors' academic success', *Social Psychology of Education*, 5, 149–77.

Chadwick, K. G. (2004), *Improving Schools through Community Engagement: A Practical Guide for Educators*. Thousand Oaks: CA Corwin.

Crossley, D. and Corbyn, G. (2006), *Learn to Transform*. London: Continuum.

Crowley, M. et al. (2007), *Qualities of Helpful Parenting: Discussion Document*. London: Parenting Education and Support Forum.

Crozier, G. and Davies, J. (2007), 'Hard to reach parents or hard to reach schools? A discussion of home-school relations, with particular reference to Bangladeshi and Pakistani parents', *British Educational Research Journal*, 33, 3.

Crozier, G., Dewey, J., Husted, T. and Kenny, L. (2000), 'Community, society and the school', *Educational Administration Abstracts*, 35, 3, 359–70.

David, M. (1993), *Parents, Gender and Education Reform*. Cambridge: Polity.

Department for Children, Schools and Families (2007), *The Children's Plan: Building Brighter Futures*.

Department of Education and Early Childhood Development

(2008), *Blueprint for Early Childhood Development and School Reform: School Reform Discussion Paper*. Melbourne, Victoria.

Fan, X. and Chen, M. (2001), 'Parental engagement and students' academic achievement: A meta-analysis', *Educational Psychology Review*, 13, 1, 1–22.

Feinstein, L. and Sabates, R. (2006), 'Does education have an impact on mothers' educational attitudes and behaviours', DfES.

Fine, M. (1993), '(Ap)parent engagement: Reflections on parents, power and urban public schools', *Teachers College Record*, 94, 4, 682–710.

Gonzalez-Dehass, A. R., Willems, P. P. and Holbein, M. F. D. (2005), 'Examining the relationship between parental engagement and student motivation', *Educational Psychology Review*, 17, 2, 99–123.

Hallgarten, J. (2000), *Parents Exist, OK!?: Issues and Visions for Parent-School Relationships*. London: Institute for Public Policy Research.

Hanafin, J. and Lynch, A. (2002), 'Peripheral voices: Parental engagement, social class, and educational disadvantage', *British Journal of Sociology of Education and Training*, 23, 1, 35–49.

Harris, A. and Chrispeels, J. H. eds (2006), *Improving Schools and Educational Systems: International Perspectives*. London: Routledge.

Harris, A. and Goodall, J. (2007), 'Engaging parents in raising achievement. Do parents know they matter?' Department for Children, Schools and Families.

Harris, A. and Goodall, J. (2008), 'Do parents know they matter? Engaging all parents in learning', *Educational Research*, 50, 3, 277–89.

Harris, A., Russ, J., Allen, T. and Goodall, J. (2007), *Reaching Out: Engaging Hard to Reach Parents*. Nottingham, LA: Nottingham.

Henderson, A. and Mapp, K. (2002), *A New Wave of Evidence: The Impact of School, Family and Community Connections on Student Achievement*. Austin, TX: Southwest Educational Development Laboratory.

Ho Sui-Chu, E. and Willms, J. D. (1996), 'Effects of parental engagement on eighth-grade achievement', *Sociology of Education*, 69, 2, 126–41.

Hoover-Dempsey, K. V., Battiato, A. C., Walker, J. M., Reed, R. P., Dejong, J. M. and Jones, K. P. (2001), 'Parental engagement in homework', *Educational Psychologist*, 36, 3, 195–209.

Hoover-Dempsey, K. V. and Sandler, H. M. (1997), 'Why do

parents become involved in their children's education?',
Review of Educational Research, 67, 1, 3–42.

Keith, T. Z., Keith, P. B., Troutman, G. C., Bickley, P. G., Trivette, P. S. and Singh, K. (1993), 'Does parental engagement affect eighth-grade student achievement? Structural analysis of national data', *School Psychology Review*, 22, 474–96.

Keith, T. Z., Reimers, T. M., Fehrmann, P. G., Pottebaum, S. M. and Aubey, L. W. (1986), 'Parental engagement, homework, and tv times: Direct and indirect effects on high school achievement', *Journal of Educational Psychology*, 78, 373–80.

Kohl, G. O., Lengua, L. J. and Mcmahon, R. J. (2000), 'Parent engagement in school: Conceptualizing multiple dimensions and their relations with family and demographic risk factors', *Journal of School Psychology*, 38, 6, 501–23.

Lareau, A. (1989), *Home Advantage: Social Class and Parental Intervention in Elementary Education*. London: Falmer.

Muller, C. (1995), 'Maternal employment, parent engagement, and mathematics achievement among adolescents', *Journal of Marriage & the Family*, 57, 1, 95–100.

Okpala, C. O., Okpala, A. O. and Smith, F. E. (2001), 'Parental engagement, instructional expenditures, family socioeconomic attributes, and student achievement', *The Journal of Educational Research*, 95, 2, 110–5.

Overstreet, S., Denivne, J., Bevans, K. and Efreom, Y. (2004), 'Predicting parental engagement in children's schooling within an economically disadvantaged African American sample', *Psychology in the Schools*, 42, 1, 101–11.

Rea, J. and Weiner, G. (1998), 'Cultures of blame and redemption – when empowerment becomes control: Practitioners' views of the effective schools movement' in *School Effectiveness for Whom? Challenges to the School Effectiveness and School Improvement Movements*, 21–32. London: Falmer Press.

Reay, D. (2000) 'A useful extension of Bourdieu's conceptual framework?: Emotional capital as a way of understanding mothers' engagement in their children's education?' *The Sociological Review*, 48, 4, 568–85.

Sacker, A., Schoon, I. and Bartley, M. (2002), 'Social inequality in educational achievement and psychological adjustment throughout childhood: Magnitude and mechanisms', *Social Science and Medicine*, 55, 863–880.

Snodgrass, D. M. (1991), 'The parent connection', *Adolescence*, 26, 83–7.

Spera, C. (2005), 'A review of the relationship among parenting practices, parenting styles, and adolescent school achievement', *Educational Psychology Review*, 17, 2, 125–46.

Sylva, K., Melhuish, E. C., Sammons, P., Siraj-Blatchford, I. and Taggart, B. (2004), 'The effective provision of pre-school education (eppe) project: Technical paper 12 – the final report: Effective pre-school education', DfES / Institute of Education, University of London.

Taylor, L. C., Hinton, I. D. and Wilson, M. N. (1995), 'Parental influences on academic performance in African American students', *Journal of Child and Family Studies*, 4, 293–302.

Vincent, C. and Martin, J. (2000), 'School based parents' groups – a politics of voice and representation', *Journal of Educational Policy*, 15, 5, 459–80.

Williams, B., Williams, J. and Ullman, A. (2002), *Parental Engagement in Education*. London: Department for Education and Skills.

Appendix 1: The Audit Tool, provided by The Compton School, Barnet

The Audit Tool provided the EPRA Strategy Group of 14 head teachers, senior leaders and academics the scaffold for developing a 'toolkit'. The EPRA toolkit is a 'one stop shop' for schools keen to develop this agenda. The toolkit provides a self-evaluation framework for schools to assess their current practice, with a guide to the types of evidence to use. The toolkit links schools to tried and tested strategies developed by schools as solutions to the challenges in overcoming barriers to parental engagement. This enables schools to set their longer-term vision for their work with parents. To access the EPRA toolkit email: engagingparents@ssatrust.org.uk

Engaging Parents to Raise Achievement

Audit Tool

Issue	Focusing	Developing	Establishing	Enhanced
1. Information (a): What information we provide for parents about the school in general				
1. Information (b): What information we provide for parents about their child				
2. Celebration: What information we provide for parents to enable them to join in celebration of success				
3. Helping learning take place: What we provide for parents to enable them to support the learning of their child				

4. Improving behaviour:
What we provide for parents to enable them to support positive behaviour

5. Extended schools and adult education:
What adult learning opportunities we provide for parents

6. Joining in:
What opportunities we provide for parents to enable them to join in the daily life of the school

Provided by The Compton School, Barnet

Appendix 2: Examples of developed practice with parental engagement from six schools

Schools on the EPRA campaign submitted case studies that recorded their work with developing parental engagement activities.

The six examples below were developed by the campaign team at the Specialist Schools and Academies Trust (SSAT) with the school leaders from each school. These examples show the profile of the schools and the activities that the schools were involved with to develop parental engagement. The campaign team worked with the school to look at the impact of this work focusing on quantitative data (from the 18 months across the campaign) and qualitative feedback. Each example concludes with recommendations and 'top tips' from the school leader.

Parental partnership at Alder Grange

School profile

- Alder Grange is a smaller than average secondary school, a non-selective school within a locality that operates a selective system.
- Students are drawn from a wide socio-economic range.
- The school is over-subscribed and all parents and carers made Alder Grange their first admission choice.
- The school's population is very stable, with a similar number of boys and girls.
- Approximately 90 per cent of the students are of White British heritage; the remaining 10 per cent are mainly Bangladeshi and Pakistani. The vast majority speak English fluently.
- The proportion of students eligible for free school meals is above the national average and there is an above average proportion of students with learning difficulties and/or disabilities, including those with a statement of special educational need.

Awards

- In 2003 the school gained specialist status in Technology.
- It has won a range of awards including: Leading Edge School, Mentor School, Listening School and Healthy School. It was re-accredited in 2006 as an Investor in People.
- The Head Teacher was voted national Head Teacher of the Year in 2004.
- In March 2007 Alder Grange became the first school in Lancashire to achieve the Leading Parent Partnership Award.

Standards and value added

- The attainment of Alder Grange students on entry is below national average and the attainment profile is skewed towards the lower ability due to the presence of selection locally.
- Standards at KS3 are in line with, or slightly above, the national average at Level 5+. This represents good value added, given the standards on entry.
- Both PANDA and the Lancashire Value Added Project show value added results that are significantly positive.
- The highest levels of value added are regularly gained by middle-ability white boys, although the differences in performance between this and other groups in school are not marked.
- GCSE results for %A*–C were above 60 per cent for the first time, results for %A*–C including Maths and English were above 50 per

cent. Results in the core subjects all improved, with an increase for maths of 20 percentage points. This represents outstanding progress given the standards on entry.

Parent partnerships

Alder Grange has always emphasized effective partnership with parents. Clare Foster, Deputy Head, believes that parental contribution really matters:

> We believe there are three basic concepts that are vital to the success of our relationship with parents:
>
> 1. Parents must be well aware of the high value we place upon their contribution.
> 2. Parents must be well aware of, and understand, our educational practice and philosophy.
> 3. We see parents as children's first 'educators', since children spend under 15 per cent of their time in school. So we need to maximize parents' effectiveness.
> 4. We aim to:
>   - make sure parents feel valued, keep them well-informed about their child's progress, involve them in decision-making
>   - support parents to work in partnership to raise their child's achievement

Clare goes on to explain that parents want to engage with school:

> No parent/carer is indifferent to school matters once they realize how vital their role could be and, as such, we have endeavored to involve parents as fully as possible by keeping them well informed about their child's progress, involving them in decision-making and giving them as much practical support as possible to work, in partnership with the school, to raise their child's achievement.

Having membership on the Strategy Group for the EPRA research project, and being one of the first schools nationally to be involved in the project, has enabled Alder Grange to remain at the forefront of educational practice and philosophy. Alder Grange works closely with colleagues across the SSAT to develop personalized learning. They have developed a whole-school approach to parental engagement, which firmly places parents at the heart of school improvement and student achievement. Mindful of the need for a coherent approach and a unified policy on parental voice and engagement, the school's strategies for parental partnership include the following:

Responsibility for engagement

A member of the senior leadership team has responsibility for engaging parents and the community, as Clare explains:

> Having a member of the senior leadership team with specific responsibility for its Parental Partnership Strategy and External Relations has enabled closer partnerships with parents, carers, and wider agencies and organizations. Regular communication with, and being accessible to, parents has reinforced the value we place on our partnership. It's also given parents an additional named contact within school who they can ask about any aspect of parental involvement.

Parental Partnership Strategy embedded in School Development Plan ... and shared with all partners

The school's Parental Partnership Strategy for 2006–2007 centred around the four EPRA themes:

- Supporting parents to help their children learn
- Personalizing provision for parents as learners
- iReporting
- Enhancing pastoral care.

This was mapped in diagrammatic form and shared with all partners.

The Parental Partnership Strategy is still based around the four EPRA themes and incorporates the objectives from the Leading Parent Partnership Award (LPPA) and the core offer for Extended Schools. As part of the future vision for parental engagement, the school has developed a systematic monitoring and evaluation process, which now forms part of the School Development Plan.

Alder Grange has 'an excellent leadership team with a strong vision for parental involvement' (LPPA).

The school's values and aims statement clearly states the value they place on their partnership with parents, and has been revisited with greater involvement and consultation from parents.

The parental partnership policy outlines the rationale behind parental partnership and offers clear guidance for how it may be achieved at Alder Grange. It has also been shared with and supported by parents.

The LPPA recognizes schools that are committed to investing in parents for the achievement of students. Clare Foster emphasizes its importance:

We believe that it's imperative for us to continue to be guided by the objectives of LPPA in order to maintain and develop effective links with parents. So our Parental Partnership Strategy for 2007–2008 is linked closely to the LPPA objectives. We found the LPPA accreditation process to be a very rewarding, reflective process, which clarified our thinking about how we want the relationship with parents to be, and how we can achieve this vision in reality. The accreditation process brought together many of our existing self-evaluation methods into a coherent, focused strategy.

Student voice

Student voice is seen by Alder Grange as instrumental in the success of any partnership with parents. All students were given a questionnaire about their perceptions of parental involvement in their education. The results were fed back to students in assemblies and to parents via the Parents' Handbook. The responses were thought provoking and proved that not everyone has the same view of what parental engagement really is.

Parents' Handbook

In September 2006, the school produced their first ever Parents' Handbook for every parent. During its production it was constantly kept in mind that information is vital – but the information parents are given must be both useful and comprehensible. The handbook, funded as part of the EPRA project, had been through a substantial period of consultation with staff, parents, students and governors. Every Child Matters (ECM) and Extended Services through Schools agendas were seen as crucial in the handbook, as Clare explains:

> The ECM agenda clearly requires that parent and family support is addressed and that organizations involved in providing services to children work together in new ways to share information and to protect children from harm. The Government is also investing in extended schools and has parenting support as one of the core offers. We used the Lancashire Supporting Parents and Families Strategy to inform us on what 'tiers' of support needed to be included within the handbook and many external agencies were also eager to contribute. Alder Grange also has membership of the Rossendale Supporting Parents and Families Forum, which has advocated and supported the handbook.

Parents' Gateway

The school introduced its online Parents' Gateway to give parents secure access to their child's data. It was envisaged that by reviewing their child's attendance and assessment grades, time-table information and conduct log, parents would effectively be 'brought into the classroom' – which would mean the capacity for much fuller participation in their child's education and have a dramatic impact upon their child's attainment and achievement.

> The quality of ICT support is both innovative and extremely open with regards to student progress information shared with parents: it is updated daily.
>
> (LPPA)

Before parents were given their user name and password for the Gateway, a Parents' Information Booklet was produced for this new technology, to make sure that parents would be able to access and understand the data provided. Information included:

- advice and frequently asked questions about Parents' Gateway
- the school's attendance policy
- the conduct log
- student assessment (an explanation of the school's academic monitoring system, the codes used for effort and progress, subject codes, rankings and information about CAT scores).

Parents without internet access were given the opportunity to go into school every Wednesday afternoon to use the system and to discuss any issues with the member of the senior leadership team who has responsibility for parental partnership.

Curriculum booklets

Curriculum booklets have now been introduced for Year 10. The aim is to produce simple and clear guidance information for all subjects on a termly basis in a consistent format that informs parents about how they can support their child's learning.

Parental Partnership evening

Alder Grange emphasizes the difference between 'parental presence' and 'parental engagement'. Every October they time-table onto the school calendar, as well as parents evenings and review days, a Parental Partnership evening, to coincide with National Parents' Week.

The evening is used as a vehicle to support the Parental Partnership Strategy. For example, past evenings have been used as a consultation evening for planning extended school activities and the programme for the school's newly built sports centre. The DfES resource 'Getting Involved' was also used in an attempt to engage parents further. In 2006, parents were told about the Parental Partnership Strategy for the coming year and the Parents' Gateway was launched during the event.

The school also offers, in partnership with Edge Hill University, accreditation for any work that parents do with their child to help raise their achievement; and partners from Edge Hill went along to the Parental Partnership evening to discuss that programme with parents.

'You said ... we did'

Alder Grange's practice of 'you said ... we did' has been very effective in their consultation with parents – and for responding to parental suggestions and concerns. Says Clare:

> At every parental engagement event we place a noticeboard in the reception area with post-it notes and pencils, and parents are encouraged to write down anything that's positive or that they feel needs to be addressed. Actions taken on these are then fed back to parents via our half-termly parents' newsletter.

Virtual School Rossendale

The school has worked even more closely with parents whose children are at risk of exclusion or in need of more personalized support. The Virtual School Rossendale (VSR) mentor has also produced information leaflets for parents to help support them with their child's behaviour.

Parents as learners

As well as courses in its community programme, the school has responded to requests from parents and held a 'Keeping Up With the Children' Modern Foreign Languages course, a 'Keeping Up With the Children' Numeracy course and a Numeracy evening. New to the offer is a Parenting course.

Feedback and future developments

Parents' Handbook

The school is currently on 'phase 2' of the Parents' Handbook, which has proved a great success. Following another period of consultation with the local high schools and special school within Rossendale, and driven by the Rossendale Supporting Parents and Families Forum and Extended Schools Officer, it has been agreed that the Alder Grange Handbook would provide the template for a Rossendale Parents' Handbook. £10,000 of funding has been secured for this through Extended Schools. Wider consultation on the handbook included the Rossendale Locality Group and the Local Strategic Partnership thematic groups, since the school felt it was important to consult with the voluntary, community and faith sectors as well as education and health groups. The handbook has been further endorsed by Lancashire County Council.

> The quality and content of the recently produced Parents' Handbook are exemplary.
>
> (Ofsted, October 2006)

'Phase 3' will look at extending the Handbook as a pilot for the next three years and to link with publications already in existence for parents within Rossendale for 0–4 years and 4–11 years; the Handbook addresses 11–16 years but plans are to extend it post-16. There are issues that still need to be addressed – for example, how to produce the handbook to meet the needs of parents whose first language is not English. In order for it to be sustainable, the school is currently investigating whether this may become a community enterprise initiative.

> Parents value the work of the school very highly. One commented, 'This school provides not just excellent teaching but is also aware of the need to develop the "whole child".
>
> (Ofsted, October 2006)

Parents' Gateway

The Parents' Gateway is building steadily, with noticeable results. Fifty-seven families (59 students) are currently using the Gateway, including 20 dads as the main user, eight students with special educational needs and one parent whose first language is Bengali.

Seventy-three per cent of the students in these families have since achieved the same attainment rank or higher; 59 per cent achieved the same or higher effort rank and 56 per cent achieved the same or higher KS3 CAT/attainment difference (the highest difference being a Year 7 boy achieving +47, whose parent requested further support with the use of the Parents' Gateway). In terms of attendance, 66 per cent improved their attendance, in many cases achieving 100 per cent. One parent, for example, whose first language is Bengali, saw her child's attainment rank increase by +11 and her effort ranking increased by +12.

- A parent with two children who both have **special educational needs** wrote: 'Thank you for the Parents' Gateway Information Booklet, username and password. I have looked at the information about the boys and have shown (name) and (name) and talked to them about their levels, effort and behaviour, etc. Actually I think it is fantastic and the information booklet is really helpful.' The boys raised their CAT/attainment difference by +23 and +15 respectively.
- A **Year 11 student** whose parent uses Parents' Gateway wrote: 'It has made a bit of a change in my behaviour and attitude. My behaviour has improved and so has my attendance and punctuality. My mum can also see what happens in the school day on Parents' Gateway. So that is why I am improving.' His attendance, punctuality and attainment ranking improved significantly, and incidences of poor behaviour decreased.

Curriculum booklet

Feedback on the curriculum booklet showed that all parents felt that it helped them understand what their child was studying that term and to support their child's learning. They also felt that it contained information that was necessary to support their child's learning. Only one parent didn't feel that it helped them to support their child's learning – but didn't give any reasons.

Parental Partnership evenings

The Parental Partnership evenings have been a great success. In 2005, 30 parents attended, more than 80 per cent being mums. The following year, more than 50 parents went along, almost a third of them dads. One parent wrote:

> I would like to say how much I enjoyed the Parental Partnership evening. I sat through your talks twice so I knew for sure that I had heard all that you both had to say and also fully understood all of the information. I found it very exciting and greatly encouraging to hear about the steps the school are taking to work in partnership with parents ... I just thought that you may like this feedback as it is obvious to me that you are sincere in wanting to improve parental involvement to enhance the children's learning potential.

Parents evenings

The school now keeps attendance lists, which they will use to target specific parents, year on year, who are not attending parents evenings.

Analysis of Parents Evenings

	Year 7 12.10.06	Year 10 1.02.07	Year 11 8.02.07	Year 9 29.03.07	Year 8 7.06.07
2005/6 overall attendance	n/a	65%	55%	67%	75%
2006/7 overall attendance	75%	66%	61%	74%	
Number in year group	132	125	140	135	
Males	72	55	76	71	
Females	60	70	64	64	
% males attendings	47%	76%	59%	76%	

Virtual School Rossendale

Four students were on VSR during the EPRA research project. Half-termly reviews with both parents and students show a positive improvement in behaviour and learning, with students being able to take greater responsibility for their own actions.

STUDENT A: Year 9 boy	PRE VSR	VSR TERM 1	VSR TERM 2
Number of exclusions	5 in year 8	2	1
Total number of days exclusion	16	6	1
STUDENT B: Year 8 boy	**PRE VSR**	**VSR TERM 1**	**VSR TERM 2**
Number of exclusions	3	2	1
Total number of days exclusion	21	6	15
STUDENT C: Year 9 girl	**PRE VSR**	**VSR TERM 1**	**VSR TERM 2**
Number of exclusions	1	0	1
Total number of days exclusion	1	0	2
STUDENT D: Year 9 girl	**PRE VSR**	**VSR TERM 1**	**VSR TERM 2**
Number of exclusions	0	0	0
Total number of days exclusion	0	0	0

Parental Partnership Strategy next stages

The school has identified a six-point plan for its next Parental Partnership Strategy stages:

1. Continue supporting parents and families to help their children learn by holding and actively promoting enrichment opportunities, events and family learning sessions that encourage joint parent/child participation – turning presence into engagement. They hope to increase engagement in parenting groups using structured evidence-based parenting programmes.

2. Further personalize provision for parents and families themselves as learners through the partnership with Edge Hill University and through the wider family learning programme.

3. Maximize new technologies and intelligent, targeted information with increased use and analysis of the Parents' Gateway, the development of the Parents' Handbook, the introduction of Parental Alert, continued roll-out of curriculum booklets and incorporating a Parents Page in the Student Planner.

4. Enhance the school environment to welcome parents and families.

5. Support and engage parents and families who are 'hard to reach' – Achievement Leaders will identify the five students who are significantly underachieving within their year group as well as the five families who are 'hard to reach'. Specific work will be done with these two groups.

6. Make a commitment to improving and evaluating the school's partnership with parents and families through continued evaluation against the objectives of the School Development Plan, the LPPA and Extended Services – and then take appropriate action. The emphasis will continue to be on the impact of parental involvement on student achievement.

Top tips from Alder Grange

- Have a member of the Senior Leadership Team with specific responsibility for parental partnership.
- Use a framework to structure your parental engagement work, for example the EPRA toolkit (available at engagingparents@ssatrust.org.uk).
- Share with all partners the importance and impact of parental engagement.
- Analyse the impact of all events and activities on student achievement.
- Embrace work with parents with enthusiasm and passion!

Access to e-portal and the Parenting Skills programme at The Compton School

School profile

- The Compton School is an 11–16 comprehensive in Barnet, serving a mixed social and economic catchment area with 21% of students on free school meals.
- The school is a Technology College and a Leading Edge school.

Standards and value added

- Students achieved 76% 5 plus A*-C grades at GCSE.
- The school's contextual value added score place it in the top 10% of schools nationally.
- At the school's third Ofsted Inspection it was judged to be 'outstanding,' achieving the highest possible accolade of grade 1s for all 24 areas inspected.

Aspirations and aims for the school's work with parents

Louise Taylor, Deputy Head, sees engaging parents as key to the school's success:

> Relationships with parents are a fundamental aspect of the success of the school. We've established a wide range of strategies for involving parents positively in the school and engaging them in the education of their children. For example, annual celebration evenings, a parenting skills support group, praise phone calls and postcards home. We wanted to explore ways of developing these relationships further and to greater effect.
>
> As a Technology College with excellent links to the local community, the school wanted to offer parents access to ICT facilities and relevant training. They introduced an e-portal and all staff have found it invaluable in terms of accessing relevant, specific and up-to-date information about students. Enabling parents to benefit from this too was an obvious next step:
>
> 'Our 'iReporting' aim is for all parents to have access to the e-portal and up-to-date data on their children. Parents will also be offered training and out-of-hours access to computers to support this.

Parenting Skills

One of the ways the school had offered support to parents was through their parenting skills support group. They trialled a six-week session with targeted parents; the SSAT project was a good opportunity to focus on expanding numbers and increasing the impact, specifically looking at:

- delivering a more focused and relevant programme of 10 sessions
- using a wider range of strategies to involve the difficult to engage parents (personalized contact by coordinator, peer support and peer recruitment, contact with other parenting groups in the local community)
- enabling parents to run the group and support each other.

Challenges and successes

The school realized that in order to enable parents to access relevant information, they had to identify precisely what information they were going to give them and how they were going to give them access to it. This inevitably raised issues to do with confidentiality. It was also important to trial the process with a specific year group before the programme was rolled out with parents across the whole school.

Supporting parental access to the e-portal

The school selected a Key Stage 3 (Year 7) and a Key Stage 4 (Year 10) group to trial the procedure. They agreed that they would enable parents to have access to all information on their child contained on the e-portal – but that they would focus on academic attainment and achievement in the e-portal training.

The training was planned to be accessible and relevant, with support by staff provided to guide parents. An accessible guide to the e-portal for parents accompanied the training and there were follow-up opportunities for parents to 'drop in' and access computers. Keen to ensure that these approaches were worth-while, the school provided strategies to evaluate the impact of their usefulness for parents and parents' frequency of use.

Supporting parental engagement through Parenting Skills

In order to provide genuine support that would enable hard to reach parents to engage in the learning of their children, the school realized that they had to identify what type of support they might find useful and find ways of offering it to them in a positive way. Consequently, they:

- Identified a member of senior leadership team to coordinate the programme
- With Heads of Year, identified the parents they wanted to target and spoke to them individually about the potential benefits of attending the sessions
- Planned a relevant and cumulative programme of 10 sessions, which focused on the role of the parent, building trust and strategies for improving parent-child relationships
- Involved parents in the planning and development of the sessions and the peer support and networking
- With parents, devised a resource pack for use by other parents
- Provided opportunities for evaluation of the impact and identification of next steps.

Outcomes in terms of impact and effectiveness

In general terms, **the e-portal system** has enabled staff to quickly identify not only individual students who need intervention but also the form that intervention should take (such as academic or pastoral). Louise explains:

> Staff are trained to ensure that parents swiftly become involved in that process by using the relevant data and information to engage and inform them of issues or concerns. Real-time information has been invaluable in improving lateness and punctuality in particular. The tutor checks daily, the Head of Year weekly and the SLT link receives a priority list every week. The specificity of the information is therefore a very powerful tool in enabling parents to identify the issues with the school and to take appropriate steps to support their child.

The parents involved in the e-portal trials have all reported that they feel confident about accessing data and information about their child and that they could use it appropriately to support the learning or behaviour needs of their child. They were confident that they could approach staff in the relevant subject or pastoral areas to provide them with further useful information. Many of them reported having looked at the information with their child and that it had provided the basis for meaningful and supportive discussions because it was accurate, relevant and up to date.

The Parenting Forum has been consistently well attended throughout the ten week programme. Some parents have attended every week, whilst others have gone along on an ad hoc basis. Parents have evaluated the impact of strategies learned by giving feedback to the group each week. The group also provided a review and evaluation to an external researcher. Without exception, parents have reported that they have felt more confident in their role as a parent because of peer support and strategies provided by the group. Parents have said that they have been able to reflect on their successes (and difficulties) as a parent and to identify ways they can help their child to build their self esteem and other strategies to develop their potential at school.

There are a number of parents from the forum who have volunteered to act as peer supports for parents who might benefit from talking individually to other parents and this informal network is now used as another strategy on offer to parents.

What next?

The school intends to complete a formal evaluation of the e-portal access and use by the trial groups so they can establish how many parents have been accessing the data and how they have used it to support their child. This will inform the way that they carry out the roll-out to the other parents. The school will also be taking part in the Parent Alerts programme with the initial trial group to provide them with a desktop notification that will alert them to relevant and up-to-date information about their child.

Parents of students involved in transition from Year 6 to Year 7 will be the focus of the parenting forum. The coordinator and volunteer parent visited feeder primary schools throughout July to collect and provide information, followed by taster sessions at the school. A revised programme tailored to support transition will then be run from September.

Top tips

Using e-portal to support parental engagement

- Ensure staff (including support staff) are confident with the data and how to communicate it effectively to parents (the individual and personalised input is crucial!) by providing ongoing training throughout the year.
- Start small and roll out gradually.
- Be selective about the information you give parents.

- Provide opportunities to review and evaluate and be flexible with next steps.

Parenting Forum to support parental engagement
- Establish a parenting coordinator who will make contact with targeted parents.
- Provide a relevant programme, which is appropriate for the specific school context.
- Build in opportunities for parents to lead, support each other, evaluate impact and suggest next steps.

Supporting students and parents at Greenford High School

School profile

- Greenford High School (GHS) is a large Foundation school in West London. The school has approximately 1140 (11–16) students, and a further 400 students in the sixth form, drawing students mainly from the local community. Almost all students live within 1.5 miles of the school, within an area that has many of the characteristics used as a basis for defining additional education need.
- Tests on students as they enter the school reveal a wide range of attainment, the majority showing standards below national average.
- Just over 20 per cent of students are eligible for free meals. 66 per cent of the school's roll is of Asian origin, 46 per cent originating from India.
- Black African students represent 10 per cent of the student population, with the biggest group from Somalia.
- Only 25 per cent of children come from homes where English is the mother tongue.
- About 7 per cent are from White heritage, 5 per cent originate from the Caribbean, and a further 1 per cent state they are dual heritage.

Standards and value added

- In 2006, 99 per cent of students gained five or more A*-G GCSE grades, with more than 67 per cent achieving 5 A*-C. Eighty per cent of students achieved grade C or better in English, and 71 per cent received C or above in Maths.
- Against prior attainment models, GHS is in the top 10 per cent at Key Stage 4, top 20 per cent at Key Stage 3; against CVA the school is in the mid range at Key Stage 4, but top 30 per cent at Key Stage 3.

Engaging parents – the focus

For GHS, involvement in the EPRA project focused on:

- **Engaging and supporting parents** to help their children learn when they transferred to secondary school – the school provided workshop sessions for parents of Year 6 transition students so that they could get to grips with the structures, expectations and curriculum of a secondary school.
- **Enhancing pastoral care** by promoting the school's unique and

innovative pastoral system. Professionals other than teachers (pastoral workers) are assigned to each year group. The accessibility and trust built up through having a full-time pastoral worker has helped the sharing of information between home and school.

- **Empowering hard to reach parents**, in part by revising the Home/School Contract. Translations and explanation have now been produced for parents whose first language is not English, and a DVD has been made in community languages for parents who can't attend in-school sessions. In particular, the school has been working with travellers, looked after children of refugees and asylum seekers, one to one and in small groups.

The approach

GHS have used a variety of approaches to make a difference in their school and beyond:

- The **pastoral structure** has been strengthened, as the non-teaching professionals (pastoral workers) take an increased role in supporting and sanctioning students.
- An **automated system to inform parents** if their children are not at school was introduced. There were initial problems with phone numbers and panicking, non-English speaking grandparents jamming the switchboard. Nevertheless, overall attendance has improved and the system has made it easier to track poor attenders. A sister system to remind parents of parents evenings and other events has also been very successful, raising the turnout to over 80 per cent in some instances.
- Introduced **consultation evenings with parents**, by year group, about the new school building and a proposed contraction to a two year Key Stage 3. Parents were told about the evenings by letter as well as the automated system, and about 20 per cent of parents took part – far higher numbers than had been anticipated and requiring on the spot room relocation.
- Provided **courses for parents** – the school had identified a particular need for parents who were struggling as their children evolved through the phases of adolescence, and could be helped by a non-judgemental support network. Jayne Ayshford, Assistant Head Teacher (Inclusion), explains:

  'We talked to an organization in a neighbouring borough that had a great deal of experience of delivering courses for parents, in both the primary and secondary sectors, and contracted with them to facilitate a course. Initially, parents were targeted through PSPs, exclusion re-integration meetings and conversations with pastoral workers, the attendance officer and other school staff. But there was an extremely poor take up on the first evening, in spite of formal applications and reminder phone calls. So we decided to postpone the remaining sessions and re-recruit. We advertized the 'Living with Your Teenager' course in the Parent Newsletter and had a slightly greater response. Overall, though, we've had disappointing results for the course.'

- Built **links with Somali** parents, which have worked well:
  'Using the already established Somali "coffee morning", we consulted parents on the educational issues they wanted to know more about. A Somali Connexions Personal Advisor worked with a focus group of Somali young people to design the content of a DVD giving parents (of children in the primary/secondary transition phase) vital information on Greenford High School in their home language. Although the Home/School agreement is translated into Somali, we are aware that many of the mothers are illiterate in their own language. Yet, in common with some of the Asian communities we work with, we know that the responsibility for the day-to-day schooling of the children falls to the mother, who often is unable to communicate in English. If there are behaviour concerns in the school, though, the father may well step in. The DVD was cast, scripted, filmed and edited by students in the Post-16 Media Department, ready for all Somali parents of children joining GHS in September.'

- **Trained pastoral staff to work with parents**, in particular through the Triple P parenting courses popular in that area of West London.

As we build our experience in working with parents, we realize how important this relationship can be to the success of our work with children and young people.

(Jayne Ayshford)

The benefits

The school is reaping the benefits of its engagement work with parents:

- A dedicated attendance officer, an automated system, and liaison with form tutors and pastoral workers have all contributed to reducing overall absence and allowed time for casework with chronic non-attenders.

- The flow of information has been speeded up, with all cause for concerns going though a pastoral system.
- Pastoral workers have an insight into the situation at home and are often able to mediate between a teacher and a student, offering an informal restorative approach and avoiding external exclusion.

What next?

The school has no intention of standing still. Jayne Ayshford outlines current and future plans:

Our reports to parents have been redesigned and represent a shift away from purely numerical reports. These new reports contain single word evaluations to be read alongside the figures – we're trialling these with the final interims of this academic year, with Year 7s only. The move into the new school buildings represents an amazing opportunity for changes. For instance, our new Virtual Learning Environment will not only be the portal for teaching and learning, but in time will be a way for parents to interact with the school and their child's education. We're also intending to produce the DVD in Polish and possibly in English too, as we recognize that for many of our parents this is a more effective communication tool than the written Home/School agreement. And we're going to look again at the requests from parents for us to provide courses for them, especially the 'Keeping Up with the Children' Maths course.

Top tips from Greenford High School

1. Listen to what the parents say – all too often we call parents because we want to 'talk to them'.
2. Develop multidisciplinary teams – recruit professionals other than teachers to work for the school.

Empowering parents at Hamstead Hall Community Learning Centre

School profile

- Hamstead Hall is an 11–18 school in the ward of Handsworth Wood. The school serves the local community of Handsworth Wood and the deprived communities of inner city Handsworth and Perry Barr.
- Handsworth and Perry Barr consist of mostly Victorian terraced houses, where urban renewal work has been carried out.
- 67.1 per cent of the ward's population come from minority ethnic backgrounds, compared with 29.6 per cent for Birmingham. These figures are reflected in the school as follows:
  - 52% – Indian
  - 23% – African-Caribbean
  - 8% – White
  - 7% – Pakistani
- 48 per cent of pupils have English as an additional language.
- 21.8 per cent of pupils have free school meals – above the national average.
- More than 14 per cent of pupils have SEN (including statements) – in line with the national average; 4 per cent have statements – above the national average.

Standards and value added

- Attainment on entry is now in line with national and LEA averages.
- Students are focused on achievement, whether academic or other. The excellent attendance of 94.3 per cent reflects the commitment of both pupils and staff alike.
- These figures were reflected in results across all levels:
  - A level: 95.4% A–E pass rate
  - GCSE: 80.4% achieving 5+ A*-C GCSEs; 99.5% achieved 1+ A*-G
  - SATs: Achieving Level 5 and above: English – 77.8%, Maths – 78.9%, Science – 64.9%
  - The school is totally inclusive and caters for all needs and abilities.
- All subjects had positive residuals for Key Stage 3 to Key Stage 4 except Music, Business and Statistics, with most performing over half a grade better than predicted. A significant strength was in Graphics, 3D Design and Art, where students achieved over a grade

better than predicted. Similar results were produced for boys and girls with weaknesses in Music and Business.

- The progress from KS2 to KS4 was excellent for Maths, with pupils, on average, achieving a grade higher than predicted and half a grade better in Science.

Empowering parents

Hamstead Hall specifically set out to:

- **Help parents understand how to support their children** to learn effectively
- **Improve opportunities of lone parents** returning to work through increased skills
- **Provide affordable childcare/extended activities** to help lone parents take up opportunities.

Parents supporting children

To help parents understand how to support their children to learn, the school set up a programme of family learning, aimed primarily at families of children with literacy difficulties. The programme also sought to find out whether parents had literacy difficulties themselves. After a pilot of four workshops early in 2006, one workshop was run monthly for eight months to enable parents to help their child at home. Each workshop lasted for two hours on a Saturday morning, at the end of which parents were given a booklet to take away, at the beginning of this was the question 'How can I help ...?'

Kate Emson, Strategic Director of Targeted and Extended Services, sees the programme as an effective way of engaging parents:

> Parents feel empowered to help their child, more confident about contacting school if there are issues, having built closer relationships with staff at the workshops. The spin-off has been that they have subsequently engaged with other family activities at the school's community club, which they saw when they attended the workshops.

Kate acknowledges that there are still issues around engaging hard to reach parents, but it is hoped this will be easier as more parents hear of the classes and become involved. Parents reported that they needed this involvement earlier in Years 6 and 7.

Reporting

The frequency of school reports has changed from one per year to one per term, and parents are given clear information on student achievement and progress. There has been parental consultation on all aspects of the reports, including surveys, letters of explanation, opportunities to respond via email, the Virtual Learning Environment or meetings. As a result, the school's Learning and Welfare directors have introduced a traffic light system so that levels of progress can be flagged to parents for further discussion. At the time of writing this report, the school was one term into discussion on a new style vertical reviewing system. Says Kate Emson:

> We will not be rushing into parental involvement. The benefits for parents missing work to attend reviews must outweigh missing time from work. We will run a small pilot with selected parents in the first instance.

Hamstead Hall has extended its targeted work with parents of black boys in Years 10 and 11 to include black boys and girls in Year 9 and black girls in Year 10. As well as their usual parents' evenings, they now also have additional evenings to support parents with Year 9 options and preparation for GCSE examinations. For Year 7 parents they have a 'settling in' evening during the first half term. All correspondence with parents is now sent through the post, on the basis that if it's important enough to write, it is essential they receive it.

Improving opportunities for lone parents

Pertemps recruitment consultants offered to attend all parents evenings and gatherings during 2006–07 to advertise skills programmes, mentoring and careers guidance that would help lone parents return to work. They also attend the school's inclusion programme on Saturdays, where single mothers bring children with disabilities to take part in activities.

The school has had 'limited success' from the parents evenings. Some parents have been signposted to college courses and are receiving mentoring related to preparation for interviews and confidence building. Input with parents attending the inclusion programme, however, has been far more successful. Following similar input from Pertemps staff, the community club has offered:

- a variety of courses to single mothers including coaching, how to run your own business, debt management and parenting skills
- work experience within the club, paid and voluntary work
- respite time, with their children being looked after and taking part in engaging activities all on one site
- transport to and from the club.

Affordable childcare/extended activities

As part of the extended schools provision, the school is only closed on public holidays. Childcare is on offer during the holidays from 8.00 a.m. to 5.30 p.m. for 28 children aged 4 to 11. Older children can take up activities throughout the holidays during the day and evening.

The school had hoped for funding for refurbishment to increase the childcare provision, but that hasn't materialised – other funding streams are being pursued. In the interim, parents are being signposted to other childcare providers and through the children's centres in the cluster.

As well as the school's community club, they have started a Teacher Free Zone (TFZ) from 3.15 p.m. to 5.15 p.m., staffed by mentors, volunteers, the school nurse and sixth formers (part paid, part volunteers) providing:

- art, homework club, internet access, guitar lessons, chill-out area, football, basketball, multi-gym, archery and – most popular – table tennis
- health drop-in for pupils and health signposting for parents
- a weigh-in for women, mothers and daughters, followed by yoga (all the health benefits plus a support for victims of domestic violence)
- a surgery run by one of the mentors to help parents with family problems, legal issues, etc., also offering targeted family support for some of the most vulnerable families.

The benefits

The benefits have been immeasurable:

- Parents know where their children are – fewer 'latchkey kids'
- Pupils are engaged in positive activities
- Less anti-social behaviour after school in the local area
- Healthier pupils – pupils with obesity are encouraged to attend
- Fills the gap between the end of school and the community club programme

- Post-exclusion pupils are directed to activities following return-to-school meetings with parents, if they are not already involved
- Child protection and LAC are offered TFZ plus transport
- Parents and students have a greater awareness of healthier lifestyles
- Parents have an improved understanding of their child's assessment information – and of their child's progress
- Parents become more engaged in the learning process
- There are more lone parents employment opportunities and greater economic well-being
- Parents have affordable childcare and activities available for their child to enable them to work.

Kate Emson is encouraged by the results:

> We have achieved a great deal over the last year and several outcomes are in line with what we would have hoped for. Others have the potential to have considerable ongoing impact, not only in engaging our parents but also engaging the wider community in the lives and achievements of our young people and their primary aged siblings.

What next?

The success of the family workshops has led to the school's involvement in Keeping Up With The Children, hosting groups from 12 local primaries and Hamstead Hall's Year 7 for a day working with their parents on health-related activities, including cooking a meal together. Says Kate:

> So far the days have been fantastic and will be followed up with four hours of literacy-focused work related to healthy food. Our feeder primary schools have sent out letters on our behalf inviting Year 5 and 6 parents to family learning workshops starting in September.

Further Adult Education classes have been set up and are open to all parents and members of the community. Parents, especially 'lone' ones, who have been involved so far will be encouraged to continue. More work opportunities will be available for parents through the community club, TFZ and other areas of extended schools.

The school has also applied to have Jobcentre Plus sited at school so that parents can look for work while their children are taking part in activities on site.

TFZ will continue to grow and hours will be extended to 6pm, so all parents will have the offer of affordable childcare.

Kate concludes:

We aim to continue with our existing good practice and extend and improve our communication and engagement with parents.

Top tips from Hamstead Hall

- Be aware of issues affecting the school and the local community.
- Be flexible with respect to times when arranging meetings with parents.
- Always have parent involvement, consultation and feedback on any new initiatives. For instance, the new head teacher shared his vision for the school with parents and invited feedback; and parents were involved in consultation for the new school uniform.

Supporting targeted groups of parents and easing transition at Kennet School

Standards and value added

- 71 per cent of students gained GCSEs at grades A*-C (including English and Maths).
- Value Added through Key Stages 2–4 = 1020.9

Aspirations

The initial aim of Kennet School's programme was to:

- extend the provision and support offered to the harder-to-reach families
- foster and improve links with parents on secondary transfer.

As the process developed, a further initiative evolved:

- working to motivate students and their families where demotivation has been impacting on attendance, self esteem and ultimately results.

The developing package of intervention involved additional staff time and support, alongside considerable involvement of parents, as Paul German, Pastoral Deputy Head, explains:

> Key to the success of the scheme has been the development of the new role of Family School Support Worker and the recruitment of an EBD/motivation support teacher within the Special Needs department. We're working to enhance their skills base and develop the range of bespoke provision. Alongside that, we have been keen to extend our already highly regarded contact with feeder primary schools and facilitate the smooth passage of certain students on secondary transfer. Again, critical to this process has been the deployment of key staff to work with named students and their families to familiarize them with the secondary school and establish high expectations from the outset.

Marlborough Group working

The development of 'Marlborough Group' working has been particularly useful. It involves running sessions in school hours (initially with specially selected Year 9 students with a variety of academic and social concerns, although this will develop).

Students and their parents undertake curriculum tasks together under the support of the group leader, a representative from the local Family Resource Team and a member of the teaching staff. This approach allows them to become familiar with the curriculum, and is an opportunity for parents to be involved and supportive, overcoming their fears in a non-threatening environment. It is followed with general discussion time and an opportunity for students to set agreed targets. Students then return to lessons and parents remain for refreshments and a critical discussion time when parenting issues are addressed. The school has found the approach extremely useful:

> It has proved invaluable, to the extent that the group pressed hard to reconvene after the normal run of six sessions for another set of parenting classes. This has enabled us to develop the programme and we plan to lead further sessions for a wider range of ages at the start of the next academic year.

It became apparent that much was to be gained from extending resources to working with students and families where disaffection has been impacting on attendance, attitude and results, so the school used a variety of data and pastoral staff referrals to determine groups within each year group (Years 7–11):

> A specialist teacher with a superb track record in developing creative solutions has been recruited, with measurably positive outcomes. Parents are regularly involved in tracking interviews and key to affecting positive change.

We have also been able to extend our impact on effective primary/secondary transfer by deploying key staff to identify with primary schools those at greatest risk of difficulty and providing bespoke support and one-to-one introductions to Kennet School for future parents and students.

The results

Motivational sessions have had a measurable positive effect with the groups in each year group targeted:

- Year 7 target group – 2.72 per cent average improvement in attendance over 3 months
- Year 8 target group – 2.28 per cent average improvement in attendance over 3 months

- Year 9 target group – 2 per cent average improvement in attendance over 3 months
- Year 10 target group – 1.25 per cent average improvement in attendance over 3 months

Parents have been interviewed and consulted throughout. Where cases have closed, rewards have been issued and letters of congratulation sent. Marlborough Group working has proved itself both by the demand for future sessions and the evaluations (verbal and written) from parents and students attending the sessions. The funding has contributed towards recruiting and deploying key staff in new roles that have had a measurable benefit to the school.

What next?

The project is set to develop further:

> Our interventions have proved positive, both from evaluations and quantitative data. Offering out-of-hours provision – such as evening courses to support parenting – has proved problematic. But this doesn't seem to have had a detrimental effect as parents have proved to be available during the day. Nevertheless, this is an area for future development within extended schools provision. We would also like to extend the developments more closely and specifically to incoming Year 7s and their families. The capacity to build more meaningful working relationships with harder-to-reach families at that stage in a secondary career has yet to be fully exploited and is a step that's planned for September 2007.

Top tips from Kennet School

1. The key resource is recruitment and staffing: creative and committed individuals have been key to initiating 'new work'.

Engaging and communicating with parents at Longcroft School and Performing Arts College

School profile

- Longcroft School and Performing Arts College is the largest and only co-educational of three 11–18 secondary comprehensive schools in Beverley, East Riding of Yorkshire. The East Riding is currently fourth in the league of poorly funded LAs in England and Wales.
- The college has 1560 students, including a sixth form of 250 students and is just completing year two of phase 2 of their specialism.

Standards and value added

- Student attainment on entry to the school is broadly average. National test results at Key Stage 3 in the core subjects have improved significantly in the last three years.
- In 2004 the school went into serious weaknesses, emerging 18 months later. GCSE results have improved significantly over the past three years. Results have moved from 52 per cent A*–C in 2004, to 72 per cent in 2007, placing them fifth in the national table for the schools with the most improved grades.
- Overall there is little difference between the results of boys and girls at GCSE. Progress in English, Mathematics and Science continues to improve and is above average at KS3 and KS4. At AS and A2, standards results are generally well above average when comparing targets to outcomes. A2 results show particularly pleasing profiles in most subjects.

Drivers for change

All staff follow the Learning and Teaching Policy, which requires differentiated work to meet the needs of all learners, and has been an undeniable driver for change, as Assistant Head Alan Cowley explains:

> The drivers for change were undoubtedly a radically altered Learning and Teaching policy, which placed increasing emphasis on accelerated learning techniques and a more robust MES (Monitoring, Evaluation and Support) programme through which we were able to control the quality of delivery more accurately. The specialism also played its part by spreading more active teaching styles across the curriculum as part of

the L&T policy implementation and by equipping several teaching areas with interactive whiteboards. There was also an unquantifiable input from reaping the twin benefits of improved communication skills in students moving up from KS3 and from the buzz that a successful performing arts college can bring. Other methods used to raise achievement were mentoring, monitoring, homework clubs, coursework clubs, extra lessons, detentions and an enormous amount of additional work, effort and stress for all staff. There was still a great amount of work being developed on ways of finding additional percentage points of improvement. Shortly after the removal of serious weaknesses, I attended an early EPRA meeting with our deputy head curriculum, where we heard some research that stated 'the single most important factor in a child's educational achievement is the home'. We made an application to be part of the funded pilot and were eventually awarded full funding.

Assessment for Learning is developing through the school and means that students and teachers can work together to identify successes and areas for development. The school has adopted Accelerated Learning techniques to ensure that students have a range of different learning opportunities catering for preferred learning styles in a coordinated way. Individual student tracking systems operate to ensure progress is monitored and intervention strategies actioned. Curriculum development in all key stages is designed to meet the needs of all. Learning routes were established in Year 7 to ensure students can work at a pace that suits their particular needs. In KS4 there is a broad range of courses on offer, including college-placed vocational experiences set within a flexible learning environment.

Engaging and communicating with parents

Longcroft's original plan had three elements and was ambitious:

1. To develop new ways of communicating with parents via the school website and other forms of electronic communication, by:
   - appointing a system manager to develop electronic registration, deliver training and manage the system
   - training teachers in its use
   - developing an e-portal
   - having meetings with parents
   - making information on the system freely available
   - teaching parents how to access system
   - developing new ways of accessing iReporting for parents without facilities at home.

2. To explore ways of informing and engaging fathers when children are underachieving, by:
   - using a database to identify underachieving students
   - identifying targeted fathers
   - inviting targeted fathers to meetings
   - establishing a control group
   - investigating ways of ensuring communications reach all fathers
   - introducing and training fathers on the system.
3. To raise student achievement by increasing parental participation and understanding of the secondary curriculum by providing differentiated support for parents so that they can help their children learn, by:
   - developing a range of curriculum information events for parents
   - holding meetings with all parents
   - making information on the system freely available
   - teaching parents how to access the system
   - the system manager co-ordinating publication of SOW and homework on the e-portal
   - subject areas designing homework tasks that invite parental involvement.

Methods

Using technology

Although the school has insisted on keeping their original targets, such has been the fascination with the project that they have not been able to resist the temptation to follow what have proved to be some exciting and fruitful developments. Alan Cowley highlights their experiences:

> There is no doubt that the e-portal is a wonderful tool but we were concerned that its use was limited to those parents with easy daytime access to a laptop or PC. We therefore investigated the possibility of extending it to use by mobile phone browsers, thus enabling a wider range of parents to access it. One of the key concerns I find in schools is finance. There can be no doubt that this impacts greatly (and frequently adversely) on the management of schools. Key to the success of this project was the data manager and such is the demand for the skills within that role that we are now on our third data manager in as many years. This has obviously had a major impact on the speed of our developments as newly appointed personnel have each had to learn the system for reporting to parents.

The second issue the school had was that they were one of the first schools in their LA to adopt the use of mobile phone technology, which was different from the one LA subsequently recommended, so there were obvious delays in retraining staff. A further issue was staff technophobia:

> Talking to other schools, I know that a commonly shared problem has been the reluctance of some teachers to embrace technology and our school has been no different in this respect. Technophobia seems to be an issue that needs to be addressed. ICT skills are best developed if they are used regularly and colleagues who are not confident in their use of ICT will naturally find reasons for using alternative methods. Staff training and support will be key in this project.

Fathers

The school was given funding by BAE for their Technology curriculum area to run a rocket club challenge for fathers and sons, which took place on a Saturday during the summer. Some families were targeted for invitation. (See also the section below on 'Parental participation'.)

Parental participation

Parental participation proved to be fundamentally the most important element of the project, since the school realized that they would have to totally change their ways of thinking, as Alan explains:

> Like the vast majority of schools, we had drifted along under the impression – gained from excellent Ofsted reports for the Community element – that everything was fine. I can now only equate this to the way schools used to feel about the issue of bullying: no one's told us there's a problem so there obviously isn't one! At a meeting we held for Year 7 parents, we found out that they were confused by the curriculum information evenings we had held and that they had found much of the written documentation sent home to be confusing too. This suggested that our efforts to engage parents of students higher up the school were failing because we had already lost much of their interest in Year 7. There was obviously a need to engage parents before transition, giving us an additional focus. (See 'Transition', below.)

As a Performing Arts College, the school has numerous performances throughout the year, appealing to a variety of tastes. But some parents still never went to any event. Alan Cowling found a solution:

> This year we organized a rock gig featuring Eddie and the Hot Rods.

This proved to be very successful as we had several parents (especially fathers) attend who we had not seen before and who we now have a channel of communication with regarding their children, some of whom have been problematic in the past. The gig also broke some stereotypes and demonstrated that we were more approachable than some parents had previously believed. We have certainly become more relevant to a wider range of parents. (The gig also showed the potential that exists for meaningful fund-raising from activities of this nature.)

Transition

It soon became apparent to the school that secondary schools quite rapidly lose the parental involvement that exists in primary school, so Longcroft looked for ways of changing this trend:

We believe that by holding simultaneous transition meetings for Year 6 students and their parents, we can ensure that parents are well briefed and that a meaningful dialogue can take place at home. Perhaps more importantly, we will be sending an important message to parents that they do have an important role to play in their child's secondary education. We are convinced that a key element in engaging parents is to establish firm relationships at KS2/3 transition. We have decided to use our specialism to achieve this and are arranging dance sessions for Year 6 students and their parents and a gospel choir purely for parents of students in partner primary schools. And as a response to those parents of Year 7 students who were not happy with the quality of information that we gave before and at KS2/3 transition, they have been asked to help write a booklet for publication in June '07 for parents of students currently in Year 6. It will be written by parents for parents, using their language. We hope that this will enable clearer communication with non-specialists and avoid such problems as the use of jargon. We also thought that two simultaneous meetings in partner schools prior to transition would be a good idea – one for students and another for parents. This will ensure that the student meetings are not dominated by parents but that both parent and child have the same information, which can then be discussed at home. It also gives a very clear message that parents are important to us in secondary education and will play a vital role in their child's continued success.

The results

The use of the database to produce accurate information for parents has been 'a great success' and the school can now supply reporting on demand if required, which Alan Cowley describes as 'very much an ongoing project for us'. They are looking forward to introducing online registration shortly, which they believe will help with student punctuality to lessons on a split-site school. They will also continue to develop opportunities for the parent voice to have a positive impact on the way that children learn and achieve.

What next?

Most individual schools may be quite happy with the current level and quality of their engagement with parents. Indeed, they may even have evidence from Ofsted to back this view. But Alan Cowley has further plans:

> Having listened to what parents had to say about parental engagement, looked now at practice in several secondary schools and it's obvious that secondary schools in particular are unwittingly presenting barriers to parental partnership through their organization and practice. One of the major barriers to parental engagement in secondary schools is an attitude that we can call 'Institutional Assumptionism'. It's an attitude that can pervade an organization (in this case schools), which communicates the message to parents that their input is not valued or wanted. The only way of tackling this is through schools committing to the professional learning of all staff. It is an issue that goes beyond teaching: Ofsted need to re-evaluate the importance of the community element of education and courses need to be developed for ITT and be included in courses in preparation for school management. As well as moving towards home or computer access for all parents.

Top tips from Longcroft School

1. Remember DAMASCUS (Don't Assume Most Adults Still Can Understand School).
2. Get parents who are not involved in education to present small pieces at Curriculum evenings.
3. Look for new ways of involving parents by using things that they're interested in.
4. Contact some parents who do not normally feel comfortable about coming in to school and ask them what the barriers are. Then do something about them.
5. Arrange to meet some parents off site in a venue they might be more comfortable with for consultation evenings.
6. Train your staff in the art of how to form working relationships with parents.